THE RECOLLECT...
Rifleman Harris

'A shepherd's tales, as told to an officer, of life in the frontline of the Napoleonic Wars prove surprisingly comestible. Describing narrow squeaks and terrible deprivations, Harris's unflowery account of fortitude and resilience in Spain still bristles with a freshness and an invigorating spikiness.'
Scotland on Sunday

'This welcome reprint of a soldier's colourful memoirs of his fighting service, mostly in Spain and Portugal during the Napoleonic wars, has been authoritatively introduced and footnoted by Christopher Hibbert.'
The Spectator

'An ordinary soldier's memoir's are rare but precious. Harris's are a most vivid record of the war in Spain and Portugal against Napoleon, the same campaign as featured in the recent TV drama series, Sharpe.'
The Mail on Sunday

THE RECOLLECTIONS OF
Rifleman Harris

AS TOLD TO HENRY CURLING

■

EDITED AND INTRODUCED BY

CHRISTOPHER HIBBERT

THE WINDRUSH PRESS · GLOUCESTERSHIRE

This edition first published in Great Britain
by Leo Cooper Ltd in 1970
Reprinted in 1996 (Twice) by The Windrush Press
Little Window, High Street,
Moreton-in-Marsh,
Gloucestershire GL56 0LL
Telephone: 01608 652012
Fax: 01608 652125

Introduction copyright © 1970, 1996 by Christopher Hibbert

British Library Cataloguing in Publication Data
A catalogue record for this book is available from the
British Library

ISBN 0 900075 64 3

The painting on the front cover is *The Rear-Guard* by J. P. Beadle.
Brig-Gen Craufurd with his rear-guard on the retreat to Vigo in
December 1808; 2nd Bn. 95th Rifles, 43rd and 52nd Light
Infantry. By kind permission of the Colonel's Commandant of the
Royal Green Jackets.

Printed and bound in Great Britain by
The Lavenham Press Ltd., Suffolk

Introduction
by Christopher Hibbert

FEW wars in the whole history of the British Army have inspired so many vivid personal records as the campaign fought against Napoleon in Spain and Portugal. In his book, *Wellington's Army*, published in 1912, Sir Charles Oman listed well over a hundred printed diaries, memoirs and series of letters, including seventeen autobiographies by non-commissioned infantrymen. Since then several other journals and collections of letters have been discovered and published. But amongst this great accumulation of material, one book remains unique. It is the *Recollections of Rifleman Harris*.

Benjamin Harris did not write the book himself. Indeed, it may be doubted that he could write at all. He told his story to Henry Curling, an officer on the half-pay of the Oxfordshire Light Infantry, who seems to have come across him long after the war was over when Harris, discharged through ill health in 1814 on a pension of sixpence a day, was working as a cobbler in Richmond Street, Soho.

Curling set the story down without much pretence to literary craftsmanship, allowing the disjointed narrative to ramble along inconsequentially; he made no attempt to correct Harris's mistakes and lapses of memory; he did not trouble to make any emendations when Harris repeated himself. But he produced a work which provides an extraordinary vivid and entirely authentic impression of what it was like to be a fighting soldier in the Napoleonic Wars.

Harris, a young shepherd from Dorset who, 'in the long winter nights', had learned the art of making shoes, was drawn by ballot for the Army of Reserve soon after its formation in 1802 and was drafted into the 66th Foot. Soldiers conscripted into the Army of Reserve could not be forced to serve outside the United Kingdom; but while with the 66th in Ireland, Harris was so captivated by the 'smart, dashing and devil-may-care appearance' of a detachment of the green-jacketed 95th Rifles he saw one day in Dublin that he volunteered to join them, and thus engaged himself for general service. Having, we can assume, been paid the normal bounty of £7 : 12 : 6, he set off on his adventurous journey 'one beautiful morning, in tip-top spirits from the Royal Oak at Cashel; the whole lot of us (early as it was) being three sheets in the wind. When we paraded before the door of the Royal Oak,' Harris goes on to relate, 'the landlord and landlady of the inn, who were quite as lively, came reeling forth, with two decanters of whisky, which they thrust into the fists of the sergeants, making them a present of decanters and all to carry along with them, and refresh themselves on the march. The piper then struck up, the sergeants flourished their decanters, and the whole route commenced a terrific yell. We then all began to dance, and danced through the town, every now and then stopping for another pull at the whisky decanters. . . . In about ten days after this, our sergeants had collected together a good batch of recruits, and we started for England.'

The 95th Rifles – which became the Rifle Brigade in 1815 – was not an old regiment and had not yet earned its battle honours; but it had already achieved a reputation which even guardsmen envied. It had been formed in the spring of 1801, following the Commander-in-Chief's order for the creation of an Experimental Rifle Corps at Horsham to which various regiments were required to send officers and men for courses of instruction. In charge of their training were two extremely able officers, Lieutenant-Colonel William Stewart and Colonel Coote Manningham; and it was as Manningham's Rifles that the 95th were first known.

In October 1802, together with the 43rd and 52nd Regiments, both of which were reconstituted as light infantry, the 95th Rifles were sent to Shorncliffe Camp on the coast of Kent to be given further specialist training by Major-General John Moore, whose exceptional gifts and nobility of character were, as one of his young officers said, 'an inspiration to us all'.

The 95th, so proud of their dark green uniforms which put concealment above show, were taught to think and to act for themselves, to combine disciplined team-work with individual initiative in a way that the British Army had never known. They were made to understand the need for their drills and exercises, not merely to perform them; they were told how to make use of ground in combining fire and movement, how to outmanœuvre the French *tirailleurs* and *voltigeurs* whose dash and skill had helped the Revolutionary armies to sweep across the plains of central Europe; they were urged to consider themselves craftsmen with a craftsman's self-respect and pride; above all, they were encouraged by example and not dragooned by fear.

They were armed not with the standard small-bore musket but with the Baker rifle. This rifle was just as liable to misfire as the musket and was even more difficult to load, as the charge had to be rammed down a rifled barrel. Few riflemen could load and fire – which they had to do standing up – in much less than thirty seconds, about twice as long as the time it took to load and fire a musket. But the rifle had one supreme advantage: the musket could not be fired accurately, even by the most expert shot, at ranges above eighty yards, whereas the rifle was accurate up to three hundred yards. Through their expertise with the rifle, their alertness, discipline and regimental pride, the 95th had become the *élite* of the Army.

Harris first saw active service with the 95th in Denmark in 1806, but he has little to say about that short campaign which, after a three days' bombardment of Copenhagen, resulted in the Danish fleet being removed from under Napoleon's nose. Nor does Harris have much to communicate about his last campaign, the ill-fated expedition to Walcheren in 1809, when four thousand of his comrades died of fever, a fever which almost killed him, too, reducing him to so pitiable a state that he was no longer fit for the life of a soldier.

Nearly all of his *Recollections* are of the war in Spain, most of them of the terrible campaign of 1809 at the end of which he stumbled down to the beach at Vigo, almost blinded by the sufferings and privations he had endured, so weak that he could stand up only with the aid of his rifle, so exhausted that he could not summon the strength to call out to the boat which was taking away the last survivors of the retreat. 'Luckily, Lieutenant Cox, who was aboard the boat, saw me, and ordered the men to return, and, making one more effort, I walked into the water, and a sailor stretching his body over the gunwale, seized me as if I had been an infant, and hauled me on board. . . . So our poor bare feet once more touched English ground. The inhabitants flocked down to the beach to see us, and they must have been a good deal surprised at the spectacle we presented. Our beards were long and ragged; almost all were without shoes and stockings; many had their clothes and accoutrements in fragments, with their heads swathed in old rags, and our weapons were covered with rust; whilst not a few had now, from toil and fatigue, become quite blind.'

Yet, for all his fearful experiences, Harris thought, as he sat at work in his shop in Richmond Street, that he 'enjoyed life more whilst on active service' than he had ever done since, and that the days spent in the fields of the Peninsula were the only part of his life 'worthy of remembrance'.

That those days at least were worthy of remembrance no one who reads the following pages could possibly deny. From the very moment that the diminutive Harris lands in Portugal and marches away under the burning sun, weighed down by his kit and great-coat, his blanket and camp kettle, his haversack, rifle, ammunition, ship-biscuit and beef, and all the tools and leather that he had to carry as the battalion's cobbler – 'the lapstone I took the liberty of flinging to the

Devil' – we know immediately that we are in the company of a natural story teller with a remarkable story to tell.

In preparing this new edition of Harris's *Recollections* for the press, I have not tampered at all with the original text. Upon the rare occasions when some additional information seems required, I have included a few explanatory words in square brackets. The footnotes provide more detailed information, particularly about the officers whom Harris mentions; but no attempt has been made to widen the scope of what is essentially a personal narrative. Readers who are unfamiliar with the military history of the period may care to read Arthur Bryant's *The Years of Victory*, Carola Oman's *Sir John Moore*, or my own *Corunna*. More detailed studies may be found in volume six of Fortescue's *History of the British Army*, volume one of Oman's *History of the Peninsular War*, and volume one of Napier's *History of the War in the Peninsula*.

CHRISTOPHER HIBBERT

PUBLISHER'S NOTE

To avoid confusion, where Harris mentions a name in the text which also appears in a footnote the spelling of the name in the text has been brought into line with that in the footnote.

1

My father was a shepherd, and I was a sheep-boy from my earliest youth. Indeed, as soon almost as I could run, I began helping my father to look after the sheep on the downs of Blandford, in Dorsetshire, where I was born. Whilst I continued to tend the flocks and herds under my charge, and occasionally (in the long winter nights) to learn the art of making shoes, I grew a hardy little chap, and was one fine day in the year 1802 drawn as a soldier for the Army of Reserve.* Thus, without troubling myself much about the change which was to take place in the hitherto quiet routine of my days, I was drafted into the 66th Regiment of Foot, bid good-bye to my shepherd companions, and was obliged to leave my father without an assistant to collect his flocks, just as he was beginning more than ever to require one; nay, indeed, I may say to want tending and looking after himself, for old age and infirmity were coming on him; his hair was growing as white as the sleet of our downs, and his countenance becoming as furrowed as the ploughed fields around. However, as I had no choice in the matter, it was quite as well that I did not grieve over my fate.

My father tried hard to buy me off, and would have persuaded the sergeant of the 66th that I was of no use as a soldier, from having maimed my right hand (by breaking a

* The Militia Act of 1802 had provided for the raising of 51,500 men by ballot. Those who could afford the current rate of £20 to £30 were allowed to pay a substitute to serve in their place. A second Militia Act, providing for the enlistment of another 25,000 men, was passed in 1803.

forefinger when a child). The sergeant, however, said I was just the sort of little chap he wanted, and off he went, carrying me (amongst a batch of recruits he had collected) away with him.

Almost the first soldiers I ever saw were those belonging to the corps in which I was now enrolled a member, and, on arriving at Winchester, we found the whole regiment there in quarters. Whilst lying at Winchester (where we remained three months), young as I was in the profession, I was picked out, amongst others, to perform a piece of duty that, for many years afterwards, remained deeply impressed upon my mind, and gave me the first impression of the stern duties of a soldier's life. A private of the 70th Regiment had deserted from that corps, and afterwards enlisted into several other regiments; indeed, I was told at the time (though I cannot answer for so great a number) that sixteen different times he had received the bounty and then stolen off. Being, however, caught at last, he was brought to trial at Portsmouth, and sentenced by general court-martial to be shot.

The 66th received a route to Portsmouth to be present on the occasion, and, as the execution would be a good hint to us young 'uns, there were four lads picked out of our corps to assist in this piece of duty, myself being one of the number chosen.

Besides these men, four soldiers from three other regiments were ordered on the firing-party, making sixteen in all. The place of execution was Portsdown Hill, near Hilsea Barracks, and the different regiments assembled must have composed a force of about fifteen thousand men, having been assembled from the Isle of Wight, from Chichester, Gosport, and other places. The sight was very imposing, and appeared to make a deep impression on all there. As for myself, I felt that I would have given a good round sum (had I possessed it) to have been in any situation rather than the one in which I now found myself; and when I looked into the faces of my companions I saw, by the pallor and anxiety depicted in each countenance, the reflection of my own feelings. When all was ready, we were moved to the front, and the culprit was

2

brought out. He made a short speech to the parade, acknowledging the justice of his sentence, and that drinking and evil company had brought the punishment upon him.

He behaved himself firmly and well, and did not seem at all to flinch. After being blindfolded, he was desired to kneel down behind a coffin, which was placed on the ground, and the drum-major of the Hilsea depot, giving us an expressive glance, we immediately commenced loading.

This was done in the deepest silence, and, the next moment, we were primed and ready. There was then a dreadful pause for a few moments, and the drum-major, again looking towards us, gave the signal before agreed upon (a flourish of his cane), and we levelled and fired. We had been previously strictly enjoined to be steady, and take good aim, and the poor fellow, pierced by several balls, fell heavily upon his back; and as he lay, with his arms pinioned to his sides, I observed that his hands wavered for a few moments, like the fins of a fish when in the agonies of death. The drum-major also observed the movement, and, making another signal, four of our party immediately stepped up to the prostrate body, and placing the muzzles of their pieces to the head, fired, and put him out of his misery. The different regiments then fell back by companies, and the word being given to march past in slow time, when each company came in line with the body, the word was given to 'mark time,' and then 'eyes left,' in order that we might all observe the terrible example. We then moved onwards, and marched from the ground to our different quarters. The 66th stopped that night about three miles from Portsdown Hill, and in the morning we returned to Winchester. The officer in command that day, I remember, was General Whitelocke, who was afterwards brought to court-martial himself.* This was the first time

* Lieutenant-General John Whitelocke (1757–1833). His incompetent direction of the attack upon the Spanish in Buenos Ayres, and his subsequent withdrawal from Montevideo, led to his being brought before a court-martial at Chelsea on 28 January, 1808. After a trial lasting seven weeks he was found guilty and sentenced to be cashiered. He spent the rest of his life in retirement.

3

of our seeing that officer. The next meeting was at Buenos Ayres, and during the confusion of that day one of us received an order from the fiery Craufurd to shoot the traitor dead if he could see him in the battle, many others of the Rifles receiving the same order from that fine and chivalrous officer.*

The unfortunate issue of the Buenos Ayres affair is matter of history, and I have nothing to say about it; but I well remember the impression it made upon us all at the time, and that Sir John Moore was present at Whitelocke's court-martial; General Craufurd, and I think General Auchmuty,† Captain Eleder of the Rifles, Captain Dickson, and one of our privates, being witnesses. We were at Hythe at the time, and I recollect our officers going off to appear against Whitelocke.

So enraged was Craufurd against him, that I heard say he strove hard to have him shot. Whitelocke's father I also heard was at his son's trial, and cried like an infant during the proceedings. Whitelocke's sword was broken over his head I was told; and for months afterwards, when our men took their glass, they used to give as a toast 'Success to grey hairs, but bad luck to White-locks.' Indeed that toast was drunk in all the public-houses around for many a day.

* Robert Craufurd (1764–1812). His reputation as a brilliant commander of light troops was established in this otherwise inglorious campaign in South America. In 1807 he was appointed to command the 1st Light Brigade in the Peninsula. This Brigade comprised the 1st Battalion of the 43rd and the 2nd Battalion of the 52nd as well as the 2nd Battalion of the 95th, in which Harris was then serving. He was killed during the siege of Ciudad Rodrigo in January 1812 and was buried in the breach through which he had led the storming party. He was a man of ferocious temper who may well have told his troops to shoot the bungling Whitelocke if they caught sight of him, although Harris did not serve in South America himself and must have learned the story second-hand.

† Sir Samuel Auchmuty (1756–1822). Before being superseded by Whitelocke he had commanded the troops in South America and had captured Montevideo. He became commander-in-chief at Madras in 1810 and commander-in-chief in Ireland in 1821.

4

Everything was new to me, I remember, and I was filled with astonishment at the bustling contrast I was so suddenly called into from the tranquil and quiet of my former life.

Whilst in Winchester, we got a route for Ireland, and embarking at Portsmouth, crossed over and landed at Cork. There we remained nine weeks; and being a smart figure and very active, I was put into the light company of the 66th, and, together with the light corps of other regiments, we were formed into light battalions, and sent off to Dublin. Whilst in Dublin, I one day saw a corps of the 95th Rifles, and fell so in love with their smart, dashing, and devil-may-care appearance, that nothing would serve me till I was a Rifleman myself; so, on arriving at Cashel one day, and falling in with a recruiting-party of that regiment, I volunteered into the second battalion. This recruiting-party were all Irishmen, and had been sent over from England to collect (amongst others) men from the Irish Militia, and were just about to return to England. I think they were as reckless and devil-may-care a set of men as ever I beheld, either before or since.

Being joined by a sergeant of the 92nd Highlanders, and a Highland piper of the same regiment (also a pair of real rollicking blades), I thought we should all have gone mad together. We started on our journey, one beautiful morning, in tip-top spirits from the Royal Oak at Cashel; the whole lot of us (early as it was) being three sheets in the wind. When we paraded before the door of the Royal Oak, the landlord and landlady of the inn, who were quite as lively, came reeling forth, with two decanters of whisky, which they thrust into the fists of the sergeants, making them a present of decanters and all to carry along with them, and refresh themselves on the march. The piper then struck up, the sergeants flourished their decanters, and the whole route commenced a terrific yell. We then all began to dance, and danced through the town, every now and then stopping for another pull at the whisky decanters. Thus we kept it up till we had danced, drank, shouted, and piped thirteen Irish miles, from Cashel to Clonmel. Such a day, I think, I never spent, as I enjoyed with these fellows; and on arriving at Clonmel we were as glorious as any soldiers in all Christendom need wish to be. In about ten days after this, our sergeants had collected together a good batch of recruits, and we started for England. Some few days before we embarked (as if we had not been bothered enough already with the unruly Paddies), we were nearly pestered to death with a detachment of old Irish women, who came from different parts (on hearing of their sons having enlisted), in order to endeavour to get them away from us. Following us down to the water's edge, they hung to their offspring, and, dragging them away, sent forth such dismal howls and moans that it was quite distracting to hear them. The lieutenant commanding the party ordered me (being the only Englishman present) to endeavour to keep them back. It was, however, as much as I could do to preserve myself from being torn to pieces by them, and I was glad to escape out of their hands.

At length we got our lads safe on board, and set sail for England.

No sooner were we out at sea, however, than our troubles began afresh with these hot-headed Paddies; for, having now nothing else to do, they got up a dreadful quarrel amongst themselves, and a religious row immediately took place, the Catholics reviling the Protestants to such a degree that a general fight ensued. The poor Protestants (being few in number) soon got the worst of it, and as fast as we made matters up among them, they broke out afresh and began the riot again.

From Pill, where we landed, we marched to Bristol, and thence to Bath. Whilst in Bath, our Irish recruits roamed about the town, staring at and admiring everything they saw, as if they had just been taken wild in the woods. They all carried immense shillelaghs in their fists, which they would not quit for a moment. Indeed they seemed to think their very lives depended on possession of these bludgeons, being ready enough to make use of them on the slightest occasion.

From Bath we marched to Andover, and when we came upon Salisbury Plain, our Irish friends got up a fresh row.

6

At first they appeared uncommonly pleased with the scene, and, dispersing over the soft carpet of the Downs, commenced a series of Irish jigs, till at length as one of the Catholics was setting to his partner (a Protestant), he gave a whoop and a leap into the air, and at the same time (as if he couldn't bear the partnership of a heretic any longer) dealt him a tremendous blow with his shillelagh, and stretched him upon the sod. This was quite enough, and the bludgeons immediately began playing away at a tremendous rate.

The poor Protestants were again quickly disposed of, and then arose a cry of Huzza for the Wicklow boys, Huzza for the Connaught boys, Huzza for Munster, and Huzza for Ulster! They then recommenced the fight as if they were determined to make an end of their soldiering altogether upon Salisbury Plains. We had, I remember, four officers with us, and they did their best to pacify their pugnacious recruits. One thrust himself amongst them, but was instantly knocked down for his pains, so that he was glad enough to escape. After they had completely tired themselves, they began to slacken in their endeavours, and apparently to feel the effect of the blows they dealt each other, and at length suffering themselves to be pacified, the officers got them into Andover.

Scarcely had we been a couple of hours there, and obtained some refreshment, ere these incorrigible blackguards again commenced quarrelling, and, collecting together in the streets, created so serious a disturbance that the officers, getting together a body of constables, seized some of the most violent and succeeded in thrusting them into the town jail; upon this their companions again collected, and endeavoured to break open the prison gates.

Baffled in this attempt, they rushed through the streets knocking down everybody they met. The drums now commenced beating up for a volunteer corps of the town, which, quickly mustering, drew up in the street before the jail, and immediately were ordered to load with ball.

This somewhat pacified the rioters, and our officers persuading them to listen to a promise of pardon for the past, peace was at length restored amongst them.

7

The next day we marched for Ashford, in Kent, where I joined the 95th Rifles, and about six months after my joining, four companies of the second battalion were ordered on the expedition to Denmark. We embarked at Deal, and sailing for the hostile shores, landed on a little place called, I think, Scarlet Island, somewhere between Elsineur and Copenhagen.*

The expedition consisted of about 30,000 men, and at the moment of our getting on shore, the whole force set up one simultaneous and tremendous cheer, a sound I cannot describe, it seemed so inspiring. This, indeed, was the first time of my hearing the style in which our men give tongue when they get near the enemy, though afterwards my ears became pretty well accustomed to such sounds.

As soon as we got on shore, the Rifles were pushed forward as the advance, in chain order, through some thick woods of fir, and when we had cleared these woods and approached Copenhagen, sentries were posted on the roads and openings leading towards the town, in order to intercept all corners, and prevent all supplies. Such posts we occupied for about three days and nights, whilst the town was being fired on by our shipping. I rather think this was the first time of Congreve rockets being brought into play, and as they rushed through the air in the dark, they appeared like so many fiery serpents, creating, I should think, terrible dismay among the besieged.†

* On Denmark's refusal to hand over her fleet until the end of the war with France, a British force was landed on Zealand and besieged Copenhagen. As Lord Grey argued at the time, the gain in ships resulting from 'this act of violence and injustice' was but 'a poor compensation' for the loss of national character and the enmity of every other power in Europe.

Harris's battalion, brigaded with the 43rd and 52nd, was in the division commanded by Sir Arthur Wellesley.

† Harris was mistaken in saying that Congreve rockets were first brought into play on this compaign. Invented by the ingenious Sir William Congreve (1772–1828), whose talents were much admired by the Prince Regent, these were first used in an attack on Boulogne in 1806.

As the main army came up, we advanced and got as near under the walls of the place as we could without being endangered by the fire from our own shipping. We now received orders ourselves to commence firing, and the rattling of the guns I shall not easily forget.

I felt so much exhilarated that I could hardly keep back, and was checked by the commander of the company (Capt. Leech), who called to me by name to keep my place. About this time, my front-rank man, a tall fellow named Jack Johnson, showed a disposition as though the firing had on him an effect the reverse of what it had on many others of the company, for he seemed inclined to hang back, and once or twice turned round in my face. I was a rear-rank man, and porting my piece, in the excitement of the moment I swore that if he did not keep his ground, I would shoot him dead on the spot; so that he found it would be quite as dangerous for him to return as to go on.

I feel sorry to record the want of courage of this man, but I do so with the less pain as it gives me the opportunity of saying that during many years' arduous service, it is the only instance I remember of a British soldier endeavouring to hold back when his comrades were going forward.

Indeed, Johnson was never again held in estimation amongst the Rifle corps; for the story got wind that I had threatened to shoot him for cowardice in the field, and Lieut. Cox mentioned to the colonel that he had overheard my doing so; and such was the contempt the man was held in by the Rifles, that he was soon afterwards removed from amongst us to a veteran battalion.

Whilst in Denmark we led a tolerably active life, the Rifles being continually on the alert – ordered hither to-day, and countermanded the next. Occasionally, too, when wanted in a hurry, we were placed in carts and rattled over the face of the country, in company with the dragoons of the German Legion;* so that, if we had not so much fighting as after-

* The King's German Legion comprised eight battalions of light infantry, two regiments of dragoons, three regiments of light dragoons as well as artillery and engineers. It had been formed

wards in the Peninsula, we had plenty of work to keep us from idleness.

Occasionally, also, we had some pleasant adventures among the blue-eyed Danish lasses, for the Rifles were always terrible fellows in that way.

One night, I remember, a party of us had possession of a gentleman's house, in which his family were residing. The family consisted of the owner of the mansion, his wife, and five very handsome daughters, besides their servants.

The first night of our occupation of the premises the party was treated with the utmost civility, and everything was set before us as if we had been their equals; for although it was not very pleasant to have a company of foreign soldiers in the house, it was doubtless thought best to do everything possible to conciliate such guests. Accordingly, on this night, a large party of the green-jackets unceremoniously sat down to tea with the family.

Five beautiful girls in a drawing-room were rather awkward companions for a set of rough and ready Riflemen, unscrupulous and bold, and I cannot say I felt easy. All went on very comfortably for some time; our fellows drank their tea very genteelly, whilst one young lady presided at the urn to serve it out, and the others sat on each side of their father and mother, chatting to us, and endeavouring to make themselves as agreeable as they could.

By and bye, however, some of our men expressed themselves dissatisfied with tea and toast, and demanded something stronger; and liquors were accordingly served to them. This was followed by more familiarity, and, the ice once broken, all respect for the host and hostess was quickly lost. I had feared this would prove the case, and on seeing several of the men commence pulling the young ladies about, kiss-

after Napoleon had overrun Hanover in 1803 and had disbanded the Electoral army, many of whose officers had come over to England. Most of its officers still were German; the ranks, though also predominantly German, had been filled up with the men of any nation – except France, Italy and Spain – willing to fight Napoleon.

ing them, and proceeding to other acts of rudeness, I saw that matters would quickly get worse, unless I interfered. Jumping up, therefore, I endeavoured to restore order, and upbraided them with the blackguardism of their behaviour after the kindness with which we had been used.

This remonstrance had some effect; and when I added that I would immediately go in quest of an officer, and report the first man I saw ill-use the ladies, I at length succeeded in extricating them from their persecutors.

The father and mother were extremely grateful to me for my interference, and I kept careful guard over the family whilst we remained in that house, which luckily was not long.

Soon after this the expedition returned to England, and I came, with others of the Rifles, in a Danish man-of-war (the Princess Caroline), and landed at Deal, from whence we had started.

From Deal we marched to Hythe, and there we lay until the year 1808, and in that year four companies of the second battalion, to which I belonged, were ordered to Portugal.

In that year I first saw the French.

2

I WISH I could picture the splendid sight of the shipping in the Downs at the time we embarked with about 20,000 men. Those were times which the soldiers of our own more peaceable days have little conception of.

At Cork, where our ships cast anchor, we lay for something like six weeks, during which time the expedition was not disembarked, with the exception of our four companies of Rifles, who were every day landed for the purpose of drill. On such occasions our merry bugles sounded over the country, and we were skirmished about in very lively fashion, always being embarked again at night.

At the expiration of the time I have mentioned our sails were given to the wind, and amidst the cheers of our comrades, we sailed majestically out of the Cove of Cork for the hostile shore, where we arrived safely [in August 1808], and disembarked at Mondego Bay.

The Rifles were the first out of the vessels, for we were, indeed, always in the front in advance, and in the rear in the retreat. Like the Kentish men of old, we claimed the post of honour in the field.

Being immediately pushed forwards up the country in advance of the main body, many of us, in this hot climate, very soon began to find out the misery of the frightful load we were condemned to march and fight under, with a burning sun above our heads, and our feet sinking every step into the hot sand.

The weight I myself toiled under was tremendous, and I often wonder at the strength I possessed at this period, which enabled me to endure it; for, indeed, I am convinced that many of our infantry sank and died under the weight of their knapsacks alone. For my own part, being a handicraft, I marched under a weight sufficient to impede the free motions of a donkey; for besides my well-filled kit, there was the great-coat rolled on its top, my blanket and camp kettle, my haver-sack, stuffed full of leather for repairing the men's shoes, together with a hammer and other tools (the lapstone I took the liberty of flinging to the devil), ship-biscuit and beef for three days. I also carried my canteen filled with water, my hatchet and rifle, and eighty rounds of ball cartridge in my pouch; this last, except the beef and biscuit, being the best thing I owned, and which I always gave the enemy the benefit of, when opportunity offered.

Altogether the quantity of things I had on my shoulders was enough and more than enough for my wants, sufficient, indeed, to sink a little fellow of five feet seven inches into the earth. Nay, so awkwardly was the load our men bore in those days placed upon their backs, that the free motion of the body was impeded, the head held down from the pile at the back of the neck, and the soldier half beaten before he came to the scratch.

We marched till it was nearly dark, and then halted for the night. I myself was immediately posted sentinel between two hedges, and in a short time General Fane came up, and himself cautioned me to be alert.*

'Remember, sentinel,' he said, 'that we are now near an active enemy; therefore be careful here, and mind what you are about.'

Next day the peasantry sent into our camp a great quantity of the good things of their country, so that our men regaled themselves upon oranges, grapes, melons, and figs, and we

* Henry Fane (1778–1840), the young commander of the light brigade in which Harris was serving. He was later transferred to the command of the 2nd Infantry Brigade, and, after a distin-guished career, became Surveyor-General of the Ordnance in 1829 at the request of the Duke of Wellington who appointed him Commander-in-Chief in India in 1835.

had an abundance of delicacies which many of us had never before tasted. Amongst other presents, a live calf was presented to the Rifles, so that altogether we feasted in our first entrance into Portugal like a company of aldermen.

The next day we again advanced, and being in a state of the utmost anxiety to come up with the French, neither the heat of the burning sun, long miles, or heavy knapsacks were able to diminish our ardour. Indeed, I often look back with wonder at the light-hearted style, the jollity, and reckless indifference with which men who were destined in so short a time to fall, hurried onwards to the field of strife; seemingly without a thought of anything but the sheer love of meeting the foe and the excitement of the battle.

It was five or six days before the battle of Roliça, the army was on the march, and we were pushing on pretty fast. The whole force had slept the night before in the open fields; indeed, as far as I know (for the Rifles were always in the front at this time), they had been for many days without any covering but the sky. We were pelting along through the streets of a village, the name of which I do not think I ever knew, so I cannot name it; I was in the front, and had just cleared the village, when I recollect observing General Hill (afterwards Lord Hill) and another officer ride up to a house, and give their horses to some of the soldiery to hold.* Our bugles at that moment sounded the halt, and I stood leaning upon my rifle near the door of the mansion which General Hill had entered: there was a little garden before the house, and I stood by the gate. Whilst I remained there, the officer who had entered with General Hill came to the door, and called to me. 'Rifleman,' said he, 'come here.' I entered the gate, and approached him. 'Go,' he continued, handing me a dollar, 'and try if you can get some wine; for we are devilish

* Rowland Hill (1772–1842). Kindly, popular and talented, he later commanded a brigade in the Hon. John Hope's division in Sir John Moore's army. He was appointed to the command of a corps during the Waterloo campaign after which Wellington expressed himself as being 'particularly indebted to him for his assistance and conduct on this as on all other occasions'.

thirsty here.' Taking the dollar, I made my way back to the village. At a wine-house, where the men were crowding around the door, and clamouring for drink (for the day was intensely hot), I succeeded, after some little difficulty, in getting a small pipkin full of wine; but the crowd was so great, that I found as much trouble in paying for it as in getting it; so I returned back as fast as I was able, fearing that the general would be impatient, and move off before I reached him. I remember Lord Hill was loosening his sword-belt as I handed him the wine. 'Drink first, Rifleman,' said he; and I took a good pull at the pipkin, and held it to him again. He looked at it as I did so, and told me I might drink it all up, for it appeared greasy; so I swallowed the remainder, and handed him back the dollar which I had received from the officer. 'Keep the money,' he said, 'my man. Go back to the village once more, and try if you cannot get me another draught.' Saying this, he handed me a second dollar, and told me to be quick. I made my way back to the village, got another pipkin full, and returned as fast as I could. The general was pleased with my promptness, and drank with great satisfaction, handing the remainder to the officer who attended him; and I dare say, if he ever recollected the circumstance afterwards, that was as sweet a draught, after the toil of the morning march, as he has drank at many a nobleman's board in Old England since.

I remember remarking Lord Hill, for the second time in my life, under circumstances which (from their not being of every-day occurrence) fixed it upon my mind. The 29th regiment received so terrible a fire, that I saw the right wing almost annihilated, and the colonel (I think his name was Lennox) lay sprawling amongst the rest.* We had ourselves caught it pretty handsomely; for there was no cover for us, and we were rather too near. The living skirmishers were lying beside heaps of their dead; but still we held our own till the battalion regiments came up. 'Fire and retire' is a very

* The Colonel of the 29th was, in fact, not Lennox but George Augustus Frederick Lake, second son of Lord Lake, Commander-in-Chief in India.

good sound; but the Rifles were not over-fond of such notes.*
We never performed that manœuvre, except when it was
made pretty plain to us that it was quite necessary; the 29th,
however, had got their fairing here at this time; and the shock
of that fire seemed to stagger the whole line, and make them
recoil. At the moment a little confusion appeared in the
ranks, I thought. Lord Hill was near at hand and saw it, and
I observed him come galloping up. He put himself at the head
of the regiment, and restored them to order in a moment.
Pouring a regular and sharp fire upon the enemy, he galled
them in return; and, remaining with the 29th till he brought
them to the charge, quickly sent the foe to the right-about.
It seemed to me that few men could have conducted the
business with more coolness and quietude of manner, under
such a storm of balls as he was exposed to. Indeed, I have
never forgotten him from that day.

At the time I was remarking these matters (loading and
firing as I lay), another circumstance divided my attention for
a while, and made me forget even the gallant conduct of
General Hill. A man near me uttered a scream of agony; and,
looking from the 29th, who were on my right, to the left,
whence the screech had come, I saw one of our sergeants,
named Frazer, sitting in a doubled-up position, and swaying
backwards and forwards, as though he had got a terrible pain
in his bowels. He continued to make so much complaint, that
I arose and went to him, for he was rather a crony of mine.

'Oh! Harris!' said he, as I took him in my arms, 'I shall
die! I shall die! The agony is so great that I cannot bear it.'

It was, indeed, dreadful to look upon him; the froth came
from his mouth, and the perspiration poured from his face.
Thank Heaven! he was soon out of pain; and, laying him
down, I returned to my place. Poor fellow! he suffered more
for the short time that he was dying than any man I think I
ever saw in the same circumstances. I had the curiosity to
return and look at him after the battle. A musket-ball, I

* Instead of the redcoats' drum, the bugle was used in rifle
regiments as a means of signalling. 'Fire and Retire' was the signal
given to skirmishers when they were too hard pressed.

found, had taken him sideways, and gone through both groins.

Within about half an hour after this I left Sergeant Frazer, and, indeed, for the time, had as completely forgotten him as if he had died a hundred years back. The sight of so much bloodshed around will not suffer the mind to dwell long on any particular casuality, even though it happen to one's dearest friend. There was no time either to think, for all was action with us Rifles just at this moment; and the barrel of my piece was so hot from continual firing that I could hardly bear to touch it, and was obliged to grasp the stock beneath the iron, as I continued to blaze away. James Ponton was another crony of mine (a gallant fellow!); he had pushed himself in front of me, and was checked by one of our officers for his rashness. 'Keep back, you Ponton!' the lieutenant said to him more than once. But Ponton was not to be restrained by anything but a bullet when in action. This time he got one; which, striking him in the thigh, I suppose hit an artery, for he died quickly. The Frenchmen's balls were flying very wickedly at that moment; and I crept up to Ponton, and took shelter by lying behind, and making a rest for my rifle of his dead body. It strikes me that I revenged his death by the assistance of his carcase. At any rate, I tried my best to hit his enemies hard. There were two small buildings in our front; and the French, having managed to get into them, annoyed us much from that quarter. A small rise in the ground close before these houses also favoured them; and our men were being handled very severely in consequence. They became angry, and wouldn't stand it any longer. One of the skirmishers, jumping up, rushed forward, crying, 'Over, boys! – over! over!' when instantly the whole line responded to the cry, 'Over! over! over!' They ran along the grass like wildfire, and dashed at the rise, fixing their sword-bayonets as they ran. The French light bobs could not stand the sight, but turned about, and fled; and, getting possession of their ground, we were soon inside the buildings. After the battle was over, I stepped across to the other house I have mentioned in order to see what was going on there, for the one

17

I remained in was now pretty well filled with the wounded (both French and English), who had managed to get there for a little shelter. Two or three surgeons, also, had arrived at this house, and were busily engaged in giving their assistance to the wounded, now also here lying as thickly as in the building which I had left; but what struck me most forcibly was, that from the circumstance of some wine-butts having been left in the apartment, and their having in the engagement been perforated by bullets, and otherwise broken, the red wine had escaped most plentifully, and ran down upon the earthen floor, where the wounded were lying, so that many of them were soaked in the wine with which their blood was mingled.

3

IT was on the 15th of August when we first came up with the French, and their skirmishers immediately commenced operations by raining a shower of balls upon us as we advanced, which we returned without delay.

The first man that was hit was Lieutenant Bunbury; he fell pierced through the head with a musket-ball, and died almost immediately.* I thought I never heard such a tremendous noise as the firing made on this occasion, and the men on both sides of me, I could occasionally observe, were falling fast. Being overmatched, we retired to a rising ground, or hillock, in our rear, and formed there all round its summit, standing three deep, the front rank kneeling. In this position we remained all night, expecting the whole host upon us every moment. At daybreak, however, we received instructions to fall back as quickly as possible upon the main body. Having done so, we now lay down for a few hours' rest, and then again advanced to feel for the enemy.

On the 17th, being still in front, we again came up with the French, and I remember observing the pleasing effect afforded by the sun's rays glancing upon their arms, as they formed in order of battle to receive us. Moving on in extended order, under whatever cover the nature of the ground afforded, together with some companies of the 60th, we began a sharp fire upon them; and thus commenced the battle of Roliça.

I do not pretend to give a description of this or any other

* Bunbury had the unfortunate distinction of being the very first British soldier to be killed in the war. He was a subaltern in the 95th.

battle I have been present at. All I can do is to tell the things which happened immediately around me, and that, I think, is as much as a private soldier can be expected to do.

Soon afterwards the firing commenced, and we had advanced pretty close upon the enemy. Taking advantage of whatever cover I could find, I threw myself down behind a small bank, where I lay so secure, that, although the Frenchmen's bullets fell pretty thickly around, I was enabled to knock several over without being dislodged; in fact, I fired away every round I had in my pouch whilst lying on this spot.

At length, after a sharp contest, we forced them to give ground, and, following them up, drove them from their position in the heights, and hung upon their skirts till they made another stand, and then the game began again.

The Rifles, indeed, fought well this day, and we lost many men. They seemed in high spirits, and delighted at having driven the enemy before them. Joseph Cochan was by my side loading and firing very industriously about this period of the day. Thirsting with heat and action, he lifted his canteen to his mouth; 'Here's to you, old boy,' he said, as he took a pull at its contents. As he did so a bullet went through the canteen, and perforating his brain, killed him in a moment. Another man fell close to him almost immediately, struck by a ball in the thigh.

Indeed we caught it severely just here, and the old iron was also playing its part amongst our poor fellows very merrily. I saw a man named Symmonds struck full in the face by a round shot, and he came to the ground a headless trunk. Meanwhile, many large balls bounded along the ground amongst us so deliberately that we could occasionally evade them without difficulty. I could relate many more of the casualties I witnessed on this day, but the above will suffice. When the roll was called after the battle, the females who missed their husbands came along the front of the line to inquire of the survivors whether they knew anything about them. Amongst other names I heard that of Cochan called in a female voice, without being replied to.

The name struck me, and I observed the poor woman who had called it, as she stood sobbing before us, and apparently afraid to make further inquiries about her husband. No man had answered to his name, or had any account to give of his fate. I myself had observed him fall, as related before, whilst drinking from his canteen; but as I looked at the poor sobbing creature before me, I felt unable to tell her of his death. At length Captain Leech observed her, and called out to the company:

'Does any man here know what has happened to Cochan? If so, let him speak out at once.'

Upon this order I immediately related what I had seen, and told the manner of his death. After a while Mrs Cochan appeared anxious to seek the spot where her husband fell, and in the hope of still finding him alive, asked me to accompany her over the field. She trusted, notwithstanding what I had told her, to find him yet alive.

'Do you think you could find it?' said Captain Leech, upon being referred to.

I told him I was sure I could, as I had remarked many objects whilst looking for cover during the skirmishing.

'Go then,' said the captain, 'and show the poor woman the spot, as she seems so desirous of finding the body.'

I accordingly took my way over the ground we had fought upon, she following and sobbing after me, and, quickly reaching the spot where her husband's body lay, pointed it out to her.

She now soon discovered all her hopes were in vain; she embraced a stiffened corpse, and after rising and contemplating his disfigured face for some minutes, with hands clasped and tears streaming down her cheeks she took a prayer-book from her pocket, and kneeling down, repeated the service for the dead over the body. When she had finished she appeared a good deal comforted, and I took the opportunity of beckoning to a pioneer I saw near with some other men, and together we dug a hole, and quickly buried the body. Mrs Cochan then returned with me to the company to which her husband had been attached, and laid herself down upon the heath near us. She lay amongst some other females, who were in the same distressing circumstances with herself, with the sky for her canopy, and a turf for her pillow, for we had no tents with us. Poor woman! I pitied her much; but there was no remedy. If she had been a duchess she must have fared the same. She was a handsome woman, I remember, and the circumstance of my having seen her husband fall, and accompanied her to find his body, begot a sort of intimacy between us. The company to which Cochan had belonged, bereaved as she was, was now her home, and she marched and took equal fortune with us to Vimeiro. She hovered about us during that battle, and then went with us to Lisbon, where she succeeded in procuring a passage to England. Such was my first acquaintance with Mrs Cochan. The circumstances of our intimacy were singular, and an attachment grew between us during the short time we remained together. What little attention I could pay her during the hardships of the march I did, and I also offered on the first opportunity to marry her. 'She had, however, received too great a shock on the occasion of her husband's death ever to think of another soldier,' she said; she therefore thanked me for my good feeling towards her, but declined my offer, and left us soon afterwards for England.

4

IT was on the 21st of August that we commenced fighting the battle of Vimeiro.

The French came down upon us in a column, and the Riflemen immediately commenced a sharp fire upon them from whatever cover they could get a shelter behind, whilst our cannon played upon them from our rear. I saw regular lanes torn through their ranks as they advanced, which were immediately closed up again as they marched steadily on. Whenever we saw a round shot thus go through the mass, we raised a shout of delight.

One of our corporals, named Murphy, was the first man in the Rifles who was hit that morning, and I remember more particularly remarking the circumstances from his apparently having a presentiment of his fate before the battle began. He was usually an active fellow, and up to this time had shown himself a good and brave soldier, but on this morning he seemed unequal to his duty. General Fane and Major Travers were standing together on an early part of this day. The general had a spy-glass in his hand, and for some time looked anxiously at the enemy. Suddenly he gave the word to fall in, and immediately all was bustle amongst us. The Honourable Captain Pakenham* spoke very sharply to Murphy, who appeared quite dejected and out of spirits, I observed. He had a presentiment of death, which is by no means an

* Captain the Hon. Hercules Pakenham (1781–1850) was the brother-in-law of Wellington, who described him as 'one of the best officers of riflemen I have seen'. He became a lieutenant-general in 1846.

uncommon circumstance, and I have observed it once or twice since this battle.

Others besides myself noticed Murphy on this morning, and, as we had reason to know he was not ordinarily deficient in courage, the circumstance was talked of after the battle was over. He was the first man shot that day.

Early on the morning of the battle I remember being relieved from picket, and throwing myself down to gain a few hours' repose before the expected engagement. So wearied was I with watching that I was hardly prostrate before I was in a sound sleep – a sleep which those only who have toiled in the field can know. I was not, however, destined to enjoy a very long repose before one of our sergeants, poking me with the muzzle of his rifle, desired me to get up, as many of the men wanted their shoes repaired immediately. This was by no means an uncommon occurrence, and I would fain have declined the job, but as several of the Riflemen who had followed the sergeant soon afterwards came round me and threw their shoes and boots at my head, I was fain to scramble on my legs, and make up my mind to go to work.

On looking around, in order to observe if there was any hut or shed in which I could more conveniently exercise my craft, I espied a house near at hand, on the rise of a small hill. So I gathered up several pairs of the dilapidated boots and shoes, and immediately made for it. Seating myself down in a small room as soon as I entered, I took the tools from my haversack and prepared to work; and as the boots of the captain of my company were amongst the bad lot, and he was barefooted for want of them, I commenced with *them*.

Hardly had I worked a quarter of an hour, when a cannon-ball (the first announcement of the coming battle) came crashing through the walls of the house, just above my head, and completely covered the captain's boot (as it lay between my knees) with dust and fragments of the building. There were only two persons in the room at the time, an old and a young woman, and they were so dreadfully scared at this sudden visitation that they ran about the room, making the house echo with their shrieks, till at length they rushed out into the open air, leaving me alone with the boots around me on the floor.

For my own part, although I was more used to such sounds, I thought it was no time and place to mend boots and shoes in, so, being thus left alone in my glory, I shook the dust from my apron, gathered up the whole stock-in-trade from the floor, and hastily replacing my tools in my haversack, followed the example of the mistress of the mansion and her daughter, and bolted out of the house. When I got into the open air, I found all in a state of bustle and activity, the men falling in, and the officers busily engaged, whilst twenty or thirty mouths opened at me the moment I appeared calling out for their boots and shoes. 'Where's my boots, Harris, you humbug?' cried one. 'Give me my shoes, you old sinner,' said another. 'The captain's boots here, Harris, instantly,' cried the sergeant. 'Make haste, and fall into the ranks as fast as you can.'

There was, indeed, no time for ceremony, so, letting go the corners of my apron, I threw down the whole lot of boots and shoes for the men to choose for themselves; the captain's being amongst the lot, with the wax-ends hanging to them (as I had left them when the cannon-ball so unceremoniously put a stop to my work), and quickly shouldering my piece, I fell into the ranks as I was ordered.

Just before the battle commenced in earnest, and whilst the officers were busily engaged with their companies, shouting the word of command, and arranging matters of moment, Captain Leech ordered a section of our men to move off, at double quick, and take possession of a windmill, which was on our left. I was amongst this section, and set off full cry towards the mill, when Captain Leech espied and roared out to me by name to return.–'Hallo! there, you Harris!' he called, 'fall out of that section directly. We want you here, my man.' I, therefore, wheeled out of the rank, and returned to him. 'You fall in amongst the men here, Harris,' he said. 'I shall not send you to that post. The cannon will play upon the mill in a few moments like hail; and what shall we do,' he continued, laughing, 'without our head shoemaker to repair our shoes?'

It is long since these transactions took place. But I remember the words of the captain as if they had been uttered but yesterday; for that which was spoken in former years in the field has made a singular impression on my mind. As I looked about me, whilst standing enranked, and just before the commencement of the battle, I thought it the most imposing sight the world could produce. Our lines glittering with bright arms; the stern features of the men, as they stood with their eyes fixed unalterably upon the enemy, the proud colours of England floating over the heads of the different battalions, and the dark cannon on the rising ground, and all in readiness to commence the awful work of death, with a noise that would deafen the whole multitude. Altogether, the sight had a singular and terrible effect upon the feelings of a youth who, a few short months before, had been a solitary shepherd upon the Downs of Dorsetshire, and had never contemplated any other sort of life than the peaceful occupation of watching the innocent sheep as they fed upon the grassy turf.

The first cannon-shot I saw fired I remember was a miss. The artilleryman made a sad bungle, and the ball went wide of the mark. We were all looking anxiously to see the effect of this shot; and another of the gunners (a red-haired man) rushed at the fellow who had fired, and in the excitement of the moment, knocked him head over heels with his fist. 'D—— you, for a fool,' he said; 'what sort of a shot do you call that? Let me take the gun.' He accordingly fired the next shot himself, as soon as the gun was loaded, and so truly did he point it at the French column on the hill-side, that we saw the fatal effect of the destructive missile, by the lane it made and the confusion it caused.

Our Riflemen (who at the moment were amongst the guns), upon seeing this, set up a tremendous shout of delight, and the battle commencing immediately, we were all soon hard at work.

I myself was very soon so hotly engaged, loading and firing

away, enveloped in the smoke I created, and the cloud which hung about me from the continued fire of my comrades, that I could see nothing for a few minutes but the red flash of my own piece amongst the white vapour clinging to my very clothes. This has often seemed to me the greatest drawback upon our present system of fighting; for whilst in such state, on a calm day, until some friendly breeze of wind clears the space around, a soldier knows no more of his position and what is about to happen in his front, or what *has* happened (even amongst his own companions) than the very dead lying around. The Rifles, as usual, were pretty busy in this battle. The French, in great numbers, came steadily down upon us, and we pelted away upon them like a shower of leaden hail. Under any cover we could find we lay; firing one moment, jumping up and running for it the next; and, when we could see before us, we observed the cannon-balls making a lane through the enemy's columns as they advanced, huzzaing and shouting like madmen.

Such is my remembrance of the commencement of the battle of Vimeiro. The battle began on a fine bright day, and the sun played on the arms of the enemy's battalions, as they came on, as if they had been tipped with gold. The battle soon became general; the smoke thickened around, and often I was obliged to stop firing, and dash it aside from my face, and try in vain to get a sight of what was going on, whilst groans and shouts and a noise of cannon and musketry appeared almost to shake the very ground. It seemed hell upon earth, I thought.

A man named John Low stood before me at this moment, and he turned round during a pause in our exertions, and addressed me: 'Harris, you humbug,' he said, 'you have got plenty of money about you, I know; for you are always staying about and picking up what you can find on the field. But I think this will be your last field-day, old boy. A good many of us will catch it, I suspect, to-day.' 'You are right, Low,' I said. 'I have got nine guineas in my pack, and if I am shot to-day, and you yourself escape, it's quite at your service. In the meantime, however, if you see any symptoms of my wishing to flinch in this business I hope you will shoot me with your own hand.' Low, as well as myself, survived this battle, and after it was over, whilst we sat down with our comrades and rested, amongst other matters talked over, Low told them of our conversation during the heat of the day, and the money I had collected, and the Rifles from that time had a great respect for me. It is, indeed, singular, how a man loses or gains caste with his comrades from his behaviour, and how closely he is observed in the field. The officers, too, are commented upon and closely observed. The men are very proud of those who are brave in the field, and kind and considerate to the soldiers under them. An act of kindness done by an officer has often during the battle been the cause of his life being saved. Nay, whatever folks may say upon the matter, I know from experience, that in our army the men like best to be officered by gentlemen, men whose education has rendered them more kind in manners than your coarse officer, sprung from obscure origin, and whose style is brutal and overbearing.

My observation has often led me to remark amongst men, that those whose birth and station might reasonably have made them fastidious under hardship and toil have generally borne their miseries without a murmur; whilst those whose previous life, one would have thought, might have better prepared them for the toils of war have been the first to cry out and complain of their hard fate.

And here let me bear testimony to the courage and endurance of that army under trials and hardships such as few armies, in any age, I should think, endured. I have seen officers and men hobbling forward, with tears in their eyes from the misery of long miles, empty stomachs, and ragged backs, without even shoes or stockings on their bleeding feet; and it was not a little that would bring a tear into the eyes of a Rifleman of the Peninsula. Youths, who had not long been removed from their parents' home and care, officers and men, have borne hardships and privations such as (in our own more peaceful days) we have little conception of; and yet these men, faint and weary with toil, would brighten up in a moment when the word ran amongst us that the enemy were at hand.

I remember on the march from Salamanca seeing many men fail. Our marches were long, and the weakly ones were found out. It was then pretty much 'every one for himself'; those whose strength began to fail looked neither to the right nor the left, but, with glassy eyes, they kept onward, staggering on as well as they could. When once down, it was sometimes not easy to get up again, and few were inclined to help their comrades when their own strength was but small. On this march, I myself (strong as I was) felt completely done up, and fell in the streets of a town called, I think, Zamora, where I lay, like one dead, for some time.

5

I T was just at the close of the battle of Vimeiro: the dreadful turmoil and noise of the engagement had hardly subsided, and I began to look into the faces of the men close around me to see who had escaped the dangers of the hour. Four or five days back I had done the same thing at Roliça. One feels, indeed, a sort of curiosity to know, after such a scene, who is remaining alive amongst the companions endeared by good conduct, or disliked from bad character, during the hardships of the campaign. I saw the ranks of the Riflemen looked very thin; it seemed to me one half had gone down. We had four companies of the 95th, and were commanded that day by Major Travers. He was a man much liked by the men of the Rifles, and, indeed, deservedly beloved by all who knew him. He was a tight hand; but a soldier likes that better than a slovenly officer.

I had observed him more than once during this day, spurring here and there, keeping the men well up, and apparently in the highest spirits. He could not have enjoyed himself more, I am sure, if he had been at a horse-race, or following a good pack of hounds. The battle was just over; a flag of truce had come over from the French; General Kellerman, I think, brought it.* We threw ourselves down where we were standing when the fire ceased. A Frenchman lay close beside me; he was dying, and called to me for water, which I understood him to require more from his manner than his words

* François Étienne de Kellerman (1770–1835), son of the Duke of Valmy. He was one of the ablest – and one of the most rapacious – of Napoleon's cavalry generals.

(he pointed to his mouth). I need not say that I got up, and gave it him. Whilst I did so, down galloped the major in front, just in the same good spirits he had been all day, plunging along, avoiding, with some little difficulty, the dead and dying, which were strewed about. He was never a very good-looking man, being hard-featured and thin; a hatchet-faced man, as we used to say. But he was a regular good 'un – a real English soldier; and that's better than if he had been the handsomest ladies'-man in the army. The major just now disclosed what none of us, I believe, knew before, namely, that his head was bald as a coot's, and that he had covered the nakedness of his nob, up to the present time, by a flowing Caxon, which, during the heat of the action, had somehow been dislodged, and was lost; yet was the major riding hither and thither, digging the spurs into his horse's flanks, and just as busy as before the firing had ceased. 'A guinea,' he kept crying as he rode, 'to any man who will find my wig!' The men, I remember, notwithstanding the sight of the wounded and dead around them, burst into shouts of laughter at him as he went; and 'a guinea to any man who will find my wig,' was the saying amongst us long after that affair.

Many a man has died in crossing a brook, it is said, who has escaped the broad waves of the Atlantic half a dozen times; the major had escaped the shot and shell of the enemy in many a hard-fought field, and came off with credit and renown; but it is somewhat singular that Punch and Judy were the individuals who were destined by the Fates to cut his thread of life, for his horse was startled one day, as he rode through the streets of Dublin city, by the clatter those worthies made with their sticks in one of their domestic quarrels, and, swerving to one side, that noble soldier was killed.

THE FAMILY OF THE COMYNS

In the band of the first battalion of the Rifles, we had a father and seven sons, of the name of Comyn. The elder son, who was called Fluellyn, was the best musician of them all, and on the regiment going on service to Portugal, he was made band-master. Whilst fighting against Massena,* Fluellyn Comyn, one night, took offence at a man named Cadogan, also belonging to our band, and, catching him at advantage, beat him so severely that he left him for dead. The transaction having been seen by some of the soldiery. Fluellyn Comyn was fearful of the consequences, and, supposing he had committed murder, fled to Marshal Massena's army, where he was received kindly, and, in consequence of his musical knowledge, promoted to a good situation in the band of one of the French regiments. After a while, however, he made some mistake or other *there*, and, the French army being no safe place for him any longer, he once more changed service, and returned amongst his old companions, the Rifles, where he found, to his surprise, Cadogan in the ranks, sound and well again. This species of inconstancy not being approved of by our leaders, he was tried by court-martial, and sentenced to be shot. Two or three other men, who had also committed heavy crimes, were under orders at the same time, I recollect, to undergo the same punishment. Colonel Beckwith was at that time our lieutenant-colonel, and, having a great respect for Comyn's father, made application to the Duke of Wellington for a pardon for his son Fluellyn. Accordingly, when he was brought forth amongst the other criminals, it was notified to him that, taking into consideration the interest made by his lieutenant-colonel, he should be forgiven: but the Duke, I understand, desired it to be expressly stated to him, that if he ever detected him in that country again, in the garb of a soldier in the British service, nothing should save him from punishment. Comyn, therefore, left Spain, without the good wish of a single man in our corps, for he was pretty well known to be altogether a bad subject. Meanwhile, the news had reached his friends in England that he had been shot, and his wife, having quickly found a substitute, was married again, when he thought proper, somewhat tardily, to seek

* André Massena, Duke of Rivoli and Prince of Essling (1756–1817), commander of the French army in the Peninsula in 1810–11.

his home. At first the meeting was rather a stormy one, and the neighbours thought that murder would ensue, for Comyn found himself provided, not only with a *locum tenens*, but also with a little baby, neither of whom he could possibly have any great liking for.

However, matters were eventually amicably arranged, and Fluellyn Comyn having made out his claim, and satisfied the second husband that he had never had a musket-ball in his body, broke up the establishment, and took his wife off to Hythe, in Kent, where he again enlisted in the *third* battalion of the Rifles, and joined them at Shoreham Cliff. In the third battalion he once more displayed his art, and, from his excellence as a musician, was made master of the band. Not satisfied with his good fortune, he again misconducted himself, and was once more reduced to the ranks. After a while he succeeded in getting exchanged to the 85th regiment, where he likewise managed to insinuate himself into the good graces of the commanding officer, and by his musical talents, also, once more, into the situation of master of the band. Here he might even yet have retrieved himself, and lived happily, but he began to cut fresh capers, and his ill-disposition and drunken conduct were so apparent the moment he got into an easy way of life, that it was found impossible to keep him in the situation, and he was again reduced, and eventually entirely dismissed, *as too bad for anything.* One of his brothers had, meanwhile, obtained the situation he held in the first battalion of the Rifles, and was greatly respected for his good conduct. He was killed, I remember, at Vittoria, by a cannon-ball striking his head from his shoulders. The other five Comyns, as far as I ever knew, lived and prospered in the service. The old father was eventually discharged, and received a pension. What was, however, the ultimate fate of the bad sheep of this flock (Fluellyn Comyn), and whether he ever succeeded in becoming a band-master in the service of any other country, or whether he ultimately reached a still more elevated situation, I never heard, but should think from all I knew and have related, that it was not likely he ever came to good.

I remember meeting with General Napier before the battle of Vimeiro.* He was then, I think, a major; and the meeting made so great an impression on me, that I have never forgotten him. I was posted in a wood the night before the battle, in the front of our army, where two roads crossed each other. The night was gloomy, and I was the very out-sentry of the British army. As I stood on my post, peering into the thick wood around me, I was aware of footsteps approaching and challenged in a low voice. Receiving no answer, I brought my rifle to the port, and bade the strangers come forward. They were Major Napier (then of the 50th foot, I think), and an officer of the Rifles. The major advanced close up to me, and looked hard in my face.

'Be alert here, sentry,' said he, 'for I expect the enemy upon us to-night, and I know not how soon.'

I was a young soldier then, and the lonely situation I was in, together with the impressive manner in which Major Napier delivered his caution, made a great impression on me, and from that hour I have never forgotten him. Indeed, I kept careful watch all night, listening to the slightest breeze amongst the foliage, in expectation of the sudden approach of the French. They ventured not, however, to molest us. Henry Jessop, one of my companions in the Rifles, sank and died of fatigue on this night, and I recollect some of our men burying him in the wood at daybreak, close to my post.

During the battle, next day, I remarked the gallant style in which the 50th, Major Napier's regiment, came to the charge. They dashed upon the enemy like a torrent breaking bounds, and the French, unable even to bear the sight of them, turned and fled. Methinks at this moment I can hear the cheer of the British soldiers in the charge, and the clatter of the Frenchmen's accoutrements, as they turned in an

* Sir Charles James Napier (1782–1853), brother of the historian, Sir William Napier (1785–1860), commanded the 50th Regiment during the retreat to Corunna. He was to achieve great fame during his command in Sind from 1842 to 1847.

instant, and went off, hard as they could run for it. I remember, too, our feeling towards the enemy on that occasion was the north side of friendly; for they had been firing upon us Rifles very sharply, greatly outnumbering our skirmishers, and appearing inclined to drive us off the face of the earth. Their lights and grenadiers I for the first time particularly remarked on that day. The grenadiers (the 70th, I think) our men seemed to know well. They were all fine-looking young men, wearing red shoulder-knots and tremendous-looking moustaches. As they came swarming upon us, they rained a perfect shower of balls, which we returned quite as sharply. Whenever one of them was knocked over, our men called out 'There goes another of Boney's Invincibles.' In the main body immediately in our rear were the second battalion 52nd, the 50th, the second battalion 43rd, and a German corps, whose number I do not remember,* besides several other regiments. The whole line seemed annoyed and angered at seeing the Rifles outnumbered by the Invincibles, and as we fell back, 'firing and retiring,' galling them handsomely as we did so, the men cried out (as it were with one voice) to charge. 'D—n them!' they roared, 'charge! charge!' General Fane, however, restrained their impetuosity. He desired them to stand fast, and keep their ground.

'Don't be too eager, men,' he said, as coolly as if we were on a drill-parade in Old England; 'I don't want you to advance just yet. Well done, 95th!' he called out, as he galloped up and down the line; 'well done 43rd, 52nd, and well done all. I'll not forget, if I live, to report your conduct to-day. They shall hear of it in England, my lads!'

A man named Brotherwood, of the 95th, at this moment rushed up to the general, and presented him with a green feather, which he had torn out of the cap of a French light-infantry soldier he had killed; 'God bless you, general!' he said; 'wear this for the sake of the 95th.' I saw the general take the feather, and stick it in his cocked hat. The next minute he gave the word to charge, and down came the

* It was the 2nd Light Battalion, King's German Legion.

whole line, through a tremendous fire of cannon and musketry – and dreadful was the slaughter as they rushed onwards. As they came up with us, we sprang to our feet, gave one hearty cheer, and charged along with them, treading over our own dead and wounded, who lay in the front. The 50th were next us as we went, and I recollect, as I said, the firmness of that regiment in the charge. They appeared like a wall of iron. The enemy turned and fled, the cavalry dashing upon them as they went off.

After the day's work was over, whilst strolling about the field, just upon the spot where this charge had taken place, I remarked a soldier of the 43rd, and a French grenadier, both dead, and lying close together. They had apparently killed each other at the same moment, for both weapons remained in the bodies of the slain. Brotherwood was lying next me during a part of this day; he was a Leicestershire man, and was killed afterwards by a cannon-ball at Vittoria. I remember his death more particularly from the circumstance of that very ball killing three of the company at the same moment, viz. Lieutenant Hopwood, Patrick Mahone, and himself. Brotherwood was amongst the skirmishers with me on this day. He was always a lively fellow, but rather irritable in disposition. Just as the French went to the right-about, I remember he d—d them furiously; and, all his bullets being gone, he grabbed a razor from his haversack, rammed it down, and fired it after them.

During this day I myself narrowly escaped being killed by our own dragoons, for somehow or other, in the confusion, I fell whilst they were charging, and the whole squadron thundering past just missed me, as I lay amongst the dead and wounded. Tired and overweighted with my knapsack and all my shoe-making implements, I lay where I had fallen for a short time, and watched the cavalry as they gained the enemy. I observed a fine, gallant-looking officer leading them on in that charge. He was a brave fellow, and bore himself like a hero; with his sword waving in the air, he cheered the men on, as he went dashing upon the enemy, and hewing and slashing at them in tremendous style. I watched for him as the dragoons came off after that charge, *but saw him no more*; he had fallen. Fine fellow! his conduct indeed made an impression upon me that I shall never forget, and I was told afterwards that he was a brother of Sir John Eustace.

A French soldier was lying beside me at this time; he was badly wounded, and hearing him moan as he lay, after I had done looking at the cavalry, I turned my attention to him, and getting up, lifted his head, and poured some water into his mouth. He was dying fast; but he thanked me in a foreign language, which, although I did not exactly understand, I could easily make out by the look he gave me. Mullins, of the Rifles, who stepped up whilst I supported his head, d—d me for a fool for my pains. 'Better knock out his brains, Harris,' said he; 'he has done *us* mischief enough, I'll be bound for it, to-day.'

After the battle I strolled about the field in order to see if there was anything to be found worth picking up amongst the dead. The first thing I saw was a three-pronged silver fork, which, as it lay by itself, had most likely been dropped by some person who had been on the look-out before me. A little further on I saw a French soldier sitting against a small rise in the ground or bank. He was wounded in the throat, and appeared very faint, the bosom of his coat being saturated with the blood which had flowed down. By his side lay his cap, and close to that was a bundle containing a quantity of gold and silver crosses, which I concluded he had plundered from some convent or church. He looked the picture of a sacrilegious thief, dying hopelessly, and overtaken by Divine wrath. I kicked over his cap, which was also full of plunder, but I declined taking anything from him. I felt fearful of incurring the wrath of Heaven for the like offence, so I left him, and passed on. A little further off lay an officer of the 50th regiment. I knew him by sight, and recognised him as he lay. He was quite dead, and lying on his back. He had been plundered, and his clothes were torn open. Three bullet-holes were close together in the pit of his stomach: beside him lay an empty pocket-book, and his epaulette had been pulled from his shoulder.

I had moved on but a few paces when I recollected that perhaps the officer's shoes might serve me, my own being considerably the worse for wear, so I returned again, went back, pulled one of his shoes off, and knelt down on one knee to try it on. It was not much better than my own; however, I determined on the exchange, and proceeded to take off its fellow. As I did so I was startled by the sharp report of a firelock, and, at the same moment, a bullet whistled close by my head. Instantly starting up, I turned, and looked in the direction whence the shot had come. There was no person near me in this part of the field. The dead and the dying lay thickly all around; but nothing else could I see. I looked to the priming of my rifle, and again turned to the dead officer of the 50th. It was evident that some plundering scoundrel had taken a shot at me, and the fact of his doing so proclaimed him one of the enemy. To distinguish him amongst the bodies strewn about was impossible; perhaps he might himself be one of the wounded. Hardly had I effected the exchange, put on the dead officer's shoes, and resumed my rifle, when another shot took place, and a second ball whistled past me. This time I was ready, and turning quickly, I saw my man: he was just about to squat down behind a small mound, about twenty paces from me. I took a haphazard shot at him, and instantly knocked him over. I immediately ran up to him; he had fallen on his face, and I heaved him over on his back, bestrode his body, and drew my sword-bayonet. There was, however, no occasion for the precaution as he was even then in the agonies of death.

It was a relief to me to find I had not been mistaken. He was a French light-infantry man, and I therefore took it quite in the way of business—he had attempted my life, and lost his own. It was the fortune of war; so, stooping down, with my sword I cut the green string that sustained his calibash, and took a hearty pull to quench my thirst.

6

AFTER I had shot the French light-infantry man, and quenched my thirst from his calibash, finding he was quite dead, I proceeded to search him. Whilst I turned him about in the endeavour at finding the booty I felt pretty certain he had gathered from the slain, an officer of the 60th approached, and accosted me.

'What! looking for money, my lad,' said he, 'eh?'

'I am, sir,' I answered; 'but I cannot discover where this fellow has hid his hoard.'

'You knocked him over, my man,' he said, 'in good style, and deserve something for the shot. Here,' he continued, stooping down and feeling in the lining of the Frenchman's coat, 'this is the place where these rascals generally carry their coin. Rip up the lining of his coat, and then search in his stock. I know them better than you seem to do.'

Thanking the officer for his courtesy, I proceeded to cut open the lining of his jacket with my sword-bayonet, and was quickly rewarded for my labour by finding a yellow silk purse, wrapped up in an old black silk handkerchief. The purse contained several doubloons, three or four napoleons, and a few dollars. Whilst I was counting the money, the value of which, except the dollars, I did not then know, I heard the bugle of the Rifles sound out the assembly, so I touched my cap to the officer, and returned towards them.

The men were standing at ease, with the officers in front. As I approached them, Major Travers, who was in command of the four companies, called me to him.

'What have you got there, sir?' he said. 'Show me.'

I handed him the purse, expecting a reprimand for my pains. He, however, only laughed as he examined it, and, turning, showed it to his brother officers.

'You did that well, Harris,' he said, 'and I am sorry the purse is not better filled. Fall in.' In saying this, he handed me back the purse, and I joined my company. Soon afterwards, the roll being called, we were all ordered to lie down and gain a little rest after our day's work.

We lay as we had stood enranked upon the field, and in a few minutes, I dare say, one half of that green line, over-wearied with their exertions, were asleep upon the ground they had so short a time before been fighting on. After we had lain for some little time, I saw several men strolling about the fields so I again quietly rose, with one or two others of the Rifles, and once more looked about me to see what I could pick up amongst the slain.

I had rambled some distance, when I saw a French officer running towards me with all his might, pursued by at least half a dozen horsemen. The Frenchman was a tall, hand-some-looking man, dressed in a blue uniform; he ran as swiftly as a wild Indian, turning and doubling like a hare. I held up my hand, and called to his pursuers not to hurt him. One of the horsemen, however, cut him down with a desperate blow, when close beside me, and the next wheeling round, as he leaned from his saddle, passed his sword through the body.

I am sorry to say there was an English dragoon amongst these scoundrels; the rest, by their dress, I judged to be Por-tuguese cavalry. Whether the Frenchman thus slaughtered was a prisoner trying to escape, or what was the cause of this cold-blooded piece of cruelty, I know not, as the horsemen immediately galloped off without a word of explanation; and feeling quite disgusted with the scene I had witnessed, I returned to my comrades, and again throwing myself down, was soon as fast asleep as any there.

I might have slept perhaps half an hour, when, the bugles again sounding, we all started to our feet, and were soon afterwards marched off to form the picquets. Towards even-ing I was posted upon a rising ground, amongst a clump of tall trees. There seemed to have been a sharp skirmish here, as three Frenchmen were lying dead amongst the long grass upon the spot where I was standing. As I threw my rifle to my shoulder, and walked past them on my beat, I observed they had been plundered, and the haversacks having been torn off, some of the contents were scattered about. Among other things, a small quantity of biscuit lay at my feet.

War is a sad blunter of the feelings I have often thought since those days. The contemplation of three ghastly bodies in this lonely spot failed then in making the slightest impression upon me. The sight had become, even in the short time I had been engaged in the trade, but too familiar. The biscuits, however, which lay in my path, I thought a blessed windfall, and, stooping, I gathered them up, scraped off the blood with which they were sprinkled with my bayonet, and ate them ravenously.

As I stood at the edge of the little plantation, and looked over to the enemy's side, I observed a large body of their cavalry drawn up. I love to call to mind the most trivial circumstances which I observed whilst in the Peninsula, and I remember many things, of small importance in themselves, and, indeed, hardly remarked at the time, as forcibly as if they had been branded into my memory. I recollect keeping a very sharp look-out at the French cavalry on that evening, for I thought them rather too near my post; and whilst I stood beneath one of the tall trees and watched them, it commenced raining, and they were ordered to cloak up.

General Kellerman and his trumpets at this moment returned to the French side; and soon afterwards, the picquets being withdrawn, I was relieved from my post, and marched off to join my company. A truce, I now found, had been concluded, and we lay down to rest for the night. Next day was devoted to the duty of burying the dead and assisting the wounded, carrying the latter off the field into a churchyard near Vimeiro.

The scene in this churchyard was somewhat singular. Two long tables had been procured from some houses near, and were placed end to end amongst the graves, and upon them were laid the men whose limbs it was found necessary to amputate. Both French and English were constantly lifted on and off these tables. As soon as the operation was performed upon one lot, they were carried off, and those in waiting hoisted up: the surgeons with their sleeves turned up, and their hands and arms covered with blood, looking like butchers in the shambles. I saw as I passed at least twenty legs lying on the ground, many of them being clothed in the long black gaiters then worn by the infantry of the line. The surgeons had plenty of work on hand that day, and not having time to take off the clothes of the wounded, they merely ripped the seams and turned the cloth back, proceeding with the operation as fast as they could.

Many of the wounded came straggling into this churchyard in search of assistance, by themselves. I saw one man, faint with loss of blood, staggering along, and turned to assist him. He was severely wounded in the head, his face being completely incrusted with the blood which had flowed during the night, and had now dried. One eyeball was knocked out of the socket, and hung down upon his cheek.

Another man I observed who had been brought in, and propped against a grave-mound. He seemed very badly hurt. The men who had carried him into the churchyard had placed his cap filled with fragments of biscuit close beside his head, and as he lay he occasionally turned his mouth towards it, got hold of a piece of biscuit, and munched it.

As I was about to leave the churchyard, Dr Ridgeway, one of the surgeons, called me back, to assist in holding a man he was endeavouring to operate upon.

'Come and help me with this man,' he said, 'or I shall be all day cutting a ball out of his shoulder.'

The patient's name was Doubter, an Irishman. He disliked the doctor's efforts, and writhed and twisted so much during the operation that it was with difficulty Dr Ridgeway could perform it. He found it necessary to cut very deep, and Doubter made a terrible outcry at every fresh incision.

'Oh, doctor dear!' he said, 'it's murdering me you are!

Blood an' 'ounds! I shall die! – I shall die! For the love of the Lord don't cut me all to pieces!'

Doubter was not altogether wrong; for, although he survived the operation, he died shortly afterwards from the effects of his wounds. After I was dismissed by the doctor, I gladly left the churchyard, and returning to the hill where the Rifles were bivouacked, was soon afterwards ordered by Captain Leech to get my shoe-making implements from my pack, and commence work upon the men's waist-belts, many of which had been much torn during the action, and I continued to be so employed as long as there was light enough to see by, after which I lay down amongst them to rest.

We lay that night upon the hill-side, many of the men breaking boughs from the trees at hand, in order to make a slight cover for their heads; the tents not being then with us.

I remember it was intensely cold during that night. So much so that I could not sleep, but lay with my feet drawn up, as if I had a fit of the cramp. I was indeed compelled more than once during the night to get up and run about, in order to put warmth into my benumbed limbs.

7

THREE days' march brought us without the walls of Lisbon, where we halted, and, the tents soon after coming up, were encamped. The second day after our arrival, as I was lying in my tent, Captain Leech and Lieutenant Cox entering it, desired me to rise and follow them. We took the way towards the town, and wandered about the streets for some time. Both these officers were good-looking men, and, in their Rifle uniform, with the pelisse hanging from one shoulder, and hessian-boots then worn, cut a dash, I thought, in the streets of Lisbon. There were no other English that I could observe in the town this day; and, what with the glances of the black-eyed lasses from the windows, and the sulky scowl of the French sentinels as we passed, I thought we caused quite a sensation in the place. Indeed I believe we were the first men that entered Lisbon after the arrival of the army without its walls.

After some little time had been spent in looking about us, the officers spied an hotel, and entering it, walked upstairs. I myself entered a sort of taproom below, and found myself in the midst of a large assemblage of French soldiers, many of whom were wounded, some with their arms hanging in scarfs, and others bandaged about the head and face. In short, one half of them appeared to carry tokens of our bullets of a few days before.

At first they appeared inclined to be civil to me, although my appearance amongst them caused rather a sensation, I observed, and three or four rose from their seats, and with all the swagger of Frenchmen strutted up, and offered to drink with me. I was young then, and full of the natural animosity against the enemy so prevalent with John Bull. I hated the French with a deadly hatred, and refused to drink with them, showing by my discourteous manner the feelings I entertained; so they turned off, with a 'Sacré!' and a 'Bah!' and, reseating themselves, commenced talking at an amazing rate all at once, and no man listening to his fellow.

Although I could not comprehend a word of the language they uttered, I could pretty well make out that I myself was the subject of the noise around me. My discourteous manners had offended them, and they seemed to be working themselves up into a violent rage. One fellow, in particular, wearing an immense pair of mustachios, and his coat loosely thrown over his shoulders, his arm being wounded and in a sling, rose up, and attempted to harangue the company. He pointed to the pouch at my waist, which contained my bullets, then to my rifle, and then to his own wounded arm, and I began to suspect that I should probably get more than I had bargained for on entering the house, unless I speedily managed to remove myself out of it, when, luckily, Lieutenant Cox and Captain Leech entered the room in search of me. They saw at a glance the state of affairs, and instantly ordered me to quit the room, themselves covering my retreat.

'Better take care, Harris,' said the captain, 'how you get amongst such a party as that again. You do not understand their language; I do: they meant mischief.'

After progressing through various streets, buying leather and implements for mending our shoes, the two officers desired me again to await them in the street, and entered a shop close at hand. The day was hot, and a wine-house being directly opposite me, after waiting some time, I crossed over, and, going in, called for a cup of wine. Here I again found myself in the midst of a large assemblage of French soldiers, and once more an object of curiosity and dislike. Nevertheless, I paid for my wine, and drank it, regardless of the clamour my intrusion had again called forth. The host, however, seemed to understand his guests better than I did, and evidently anticipated mischief. After in vain trying to make me understand him, he suddenly jumped from behind his bar, and seizing me by the shoulder without ceremony, thrust me into the street. I found the two officers looking anxiously for me when I got out, and not quite easy at my disappearance. I, however, excused myself by pleading the heat of the day, and my anxiety to taste the good wines of Lisbon, and together we left the town, with our purchases, and reached the camp.

Next morning Captain Leech again entered my tent, and desired me to pick out three good workmen from the company, take them into the town, and seek out a shoemaker's shop as near the camp as possible.

'You must get leave to work in the first shop you can find,' he said, 'as we have a long march before us, and many of the men without shoes to their feet.'

Accordingly, we carried with us three small sacks filled with old boots and shoes, and entering Lisbon went into the first shoemaker's shop we saw. Here I endeavoured in vain to make myself understood for some time. There was a master shoemaker at work and three men. They did not seem to like our intrusion, and looked very sulky, asking us various questions, which I could not understand; the only words I could at all comprehend being 'Bonos Irelandos, Brutu Englisa.' I thought, considering we had come so far to fight their battles for them, that this was the north side of civil; so I signed to the men, and, by way of explanation of our wishes, and in order to cut the matter short, they emptied the three sacksful of boots and shoes upon the floor. We now explained what we would be at; the boots and shoes of the Rifles spoke for themselves, and, seating ourselves, we commenced work forthwith.

In this way we continued employed whilst the army lay near Lisbon, every morning coming in to work, and returning to the camp every night to sleep.

After we had been there several days, our landlord's family had the curiosity to come occasionally and take a peep at us. My companions were noisy, good-tempered, jolly fellows, and usually sang all the time they hammered and strapped. The mistress of the house, seeing I was the head man, occasionally came and sat down beside me as I worked, bringing her daughter, a very handsome dark-eyed Spanish girl, and as a matter of course I fell in love.

We soon became better acquainted, and the mother, one evening, after having sat and chattered to me, serving me with wine, and other good things, on my rising to leave the shop, made a signal for me to follow her. She had managed to pick up a little English, and I knew a few words of the Spanish language, so that we could pretty well comprehend each other's meaning; and after leading me into their sitting-room, she brought her handsome daughter, and, without more circumstance, offered her to me for a wife. The offer was a tempting one; but the conditions of the marriage made it impossible for me to comply, since I was to change my religion, and desert my colours. The old dame proposed to conceal me effectually when the army marched; after which I was to live like a gentleman, with the handsome Maria for a wife.

It was hard to refuse so tempting an offer, with the pretty Maria endeavouring to back her mother's proposal. I, however, made them understand that nothing would tempt me to desert; and, promising to try and get my discharge when I returned to England, protested I would then return and marry Maria.

Soon after this the army marched for Spain; the Rifles paraded in the very street where the shop I had so long worked at was situated, and I saw Maria at the window. As our bugles struck up, she waved her handkerchief; I returned the salute, and in half an hour had forgotten all about her. So much for a soldier's love. Our marches were now long and fatiguing. I do not know how many miles we traversed ere we reached Almeida, which I was told was the last town in Portugal: some of my companions said we had come five hundred miles since we left Lisbon.

We now passed to the left, and bade adieu to Portugal for ever. We had fought and conquered, and felt elated accordingly. Spain was before us, and every man in the Rifles seemed only anxious to get a rap at the French again. On and on we toiled, till we reached Salamanca. I love to remember the appearance of that army, as we moved along at this time. It was a glorious sight to see our colours spread in these fields. The men seemed invincible; nothing, I thought, could have beaten them. We had some of as desperate fellows in the Rifles alone as had ever toiled under the burning sun of an enemy's country in any age; but I lived to see hardship and toil lay hundreds of them low, before a few weeks were over our heads. At Salamanca we stayed seven or eight days, and during this time the shoemakers were again wanted, and I worked with my men incessantly during their short halt.

Our marches were now still more arduous; fourteen leagues a day, I have heard the men say, we accomplished before we halted; and many of us were found out, and floored in the road.* It became every one for himself. The load we carried was too great, and we staggered on, looking neither to the right nor the left. If a man dropped, he found it no easy matter to get up again, unless his companion assisted him, and many died of fatigue. As for myself, I was nearly floored by this march; and on reaching a town one night, which I think was called Zamora, I fell at the entrance of the first street we came to; the sight left my eyes, my brain reeled, and I came down like a dead man. When I recovered my senses, I remember that I crawled into a door I found open, and, being too ill to rise, lay for some time in the passage unregarded by the inhabitants.

After I had left the house I have alluded to in the account of the battle of Roliça, I walked a few paces onwards, when I saw some of the Rifles lying about and resting. I laid myself down amongst them, for I felt fatigued. A great many of the French skirmishers were lying dead just about this spot. I recollect that they had long white frockcoats on, with the

* This is probably not so gross an exaggeration as it appears. Forty-two miles a day seems extraordinary for soldiers so heavily encumbered. But it is a matter of fact that General the Hon. John Hope's division marched forty-seven miles to Peñaranda in the first thirty-six hours of December, 1808.

eagle in front of their caps. This was one of the places from which they had greatly annoyed us; and, to judge from the appearance of the dead and wounded strewed around, we had returned the compliment pretty handsomely. I lay upon my back, and, resting upon my knapsack, examined the enemy in the distance. Their lines were about a couple of miles off : here they remained stationary, I should think, until near sunset, when they began to vanish, beating towards Vimeiro, where we had at them again. Whilst I lay watching them, I observed a dead man directly opposite to me whose singular appearance had not at first caught my eye. He was lying on his side amongst some burnt-up bushes; and whether the heat of the firing here had set these bushes on fire, or from whatever cause they had been ignited, I cannot take upon me to say; but certain it is (for several of my companions saw it as well as myself, and cracked many a joke upon the poor fellow's appearance) that this man, whom we guessed to have been French, was as completely roasted as if he had been spitted before a good kitchen fire. He was burnt quite brown, every stitch of clothes was singed off, and he was drawn all up like a dried frog. I called the attention of one or two men near me, and we examined him, turning him about with our rifles with no little curiosity. I remember now, with some surprise, that the miserable fate of this poor fellow called forth from us very little sympathy, but seemed only to be a subject of mirth.

8

I REMEMBER there was an officer, named, I think, Cardo, with the Rifles.* He was a great beau; but although rather effeminate and ladylike in manners, so much so as to be remarked by the whole regiment at that time, yet he was found to be a most gallant officer when we were engaged with the enemy in the field.

He was killed whilst fighting bravely in the Pyrenees; and amongst other jewellery he wore, he had a ring on his finger worth one hundred and fifty guineas.

As he lay dead on the field, one of our Riflemen, named Orr, observed the sparkling gem, and immediately resolved to make prize of it. The ring, however, was so firmly fixed that Orr could not draw it from the finger, and whipping out his knife cut the finger off by the joint. After the battle Orr offered the ring for sale amongst the officers, and, on inquiry, the manner in which he had obtained it transpired. Orr was in consequence tried by court-martial, and sentenced to receive five hundred lashes, which sentence was carried into execution.

A youth joined the Rifles soon after I myself put on the green jacket, whose name was Medley. He was but a small chap, being under the standard one inch;† but our officers thought he promised fair to become a tall fellow, and he was, accordingly, not rejected. Medley did not deceive them; for,

* Harris refers to Daniel Cadour who was killed at Pamplona.
† Riflemen at this time were required to be at least 5 ft. 2 ins. tall.

on the day he first joined the Rifles, he was five feet one inch in height, and on the day he was killed, at Barrossa, he was exactly six feet one. He was celebrated for being the greatest grumbler, the greatest eater, and the most quarrelsome fellow in the whole corps. I remember he cut a most desperate figure in the retreat to Coruña; for there he had enough to bear both of fatigue and hunger; and a very little of either of these disagreeables would make him extremely bad company at any time. It was dangerous, too, to bid him hold his tongue sometimes; for he had picked up so amongst us since he was only five feet one, and grown so bony as well as tall, that he would challenge and thrash any man in the corps. Coruña, however, though it could not stop his growling, took the desire of boxing quite out of him; and he sprawled, scrambled, and swore, till he somehow got through that business. If General Craufurd could have heard but the twentieth part of what I heard him utter about him on that retreat, I think he would have cut Medley in half. He was, as I said, a capital feeder; and his own allowance was not half enough to satisfy his cravings, so that he often got some of his comrades to help him out with a portion of theirs. He was my comrade for about two years; and, as I was a shoemaker, I often had food to give him; indeed it was highly necessary either to give him what I had for my own allowance, or find some provision elsewhere, for he was the most cross-grained fellow, if his belly was not filled, that we ever had amongst us. He was killed at Barrossa, as I said, and he carried his ill-humour with him to the very last hour of his life; for, being knocked over by a musket-ball in the thigh, he was spoken to as he lay by some of his comrades, who, asking if they should assist him, and carry him to the rear, he told them to 'Go and be d—d!' and, bidding them mind their own business, abused them till they passed on and left him. I was told this last anecdote of him by the very men who had spoken to him, and got this blessing as he lay.

We had another tall fellow in the four companies of Rifles who were in that retreat. His name was Thomas Higgins; he was six feet one and a half, and quite as lank and bony as

Medley. He also was an ill-tempered fellow, but nothing to compare with him either in eating or grumbling. The tall men, I have often observed, bore fatigue much worse than the short ones; and Higgins, amongst others of the big 'uns, was dreadfully put to it to keep on. We lost him entirely when about half through this business, I remember, for, during a short halt of about ten minutes, he was reprimanded by one of our officers for the slovenly state of his clothing and accoutrements; his dress almost dropping from his lower limbs, and his knapsack hanging by a strap or two down about his waist. Higgins did not take it at all kind being quarrelled with at such a time, and, uttering sundry impertinences, desired to know if they were ever to be allowed to halt any more, adding that he did not see very well how he was to be very smart after what he had already gone through. The officer spoke to one of the sergeants upon this, and bid him remember, if they got to their journey's end, to give Higgins an extra guard for his behaviour. 'Oh! then, d—n me,' says Higgins, 'if ever I take it!' and, turning about, as we all moved on at the word to march, he marched off in the contrary direction, and we never either saw or heard of him from that hour; and it was supposed afterwards amongst us, that he had either perished alone in the night, or joined the French, who were at our heels. These were the two tallest men in the four companies of Rifles; and both were in the company I belonged to. Higgins was the right-hand, and Medley the left-hand man.

THE YORKSHIRE FARMER

It was about the year 1807 or 1808 that a man volunteered from the Nottingham Militia into the Rifles. After receiving the half of his bounty, he thought that was quite as much as would serve him of the Rifle regiment, and so he declined to serve them in return, and accordingly made off, without joining them at all at that time. Four years afterwards he was discovered by the very sergeant of the Nottingham Militia who belonged to his own company when he volunteered from them into our corps. This same sergeant was then himself recruiting, and fell in with his former comrade in some town, of which I forget the name; but it was in Yorkshire. The man (whose name, also, I have forgotten now) was then grown very fat, and was, likewise, as much altered in dress as in condition, being clad in the habiliments of a respectable and comfortable farmer of that delightful county. The sergeant, however, had a sharp eye, and penetrated both through the disguise of his then calling, and also even his portly look failed in throwing him off the scent. In fact, he went warily to work, made his inquiries, compared his notes, allowed for the time and circumstances, and, notwithstanding the respectability and reputed worth of our farmer, arrested him forthwith as a deserter from the 95th. From Yorkshire he was marched a prisoner to Hythe, in Kent; and I remember seeing him brought in, dressed as he was apprehended, and handcuffed, and guarded by a corporal and three or four men. He was, as I said, clad in his farmer's dress, and that it was which made myself and others (who happened to be out) more especially regard him; for, although it was no great sight at that time to see a deserter brought along, yet it was not often we beheld one so apparently well off and respectable-looking in such a situation. In fact, the Yorkshire farmer made a great talk amongst us; and we pitied him much. No man in his present circumstances could, I should think, feel more acutely, and he dwindled perceptibly in bulk every day, till he was brought to trial. During his confinement he had written to the colonel of the regiment offering him sixty pounds to let him off; but I believe he never at that time got any reply to his offer, and, being tried, was sentenced to receive seven hundred lashes. When he was brought into the hollow square to receive his punishment, I remember the anxiety amongst us was twice as great as on an ordinary occasion of the sort. He did not seem a man who was afraid of the lash, as regarded the pain of its infliction, but the shame of it (considering the situation he had attained to) was apparently the thing that hurt him most. Even now, although fallen away, he was a jolly and portly-looking man, though his flesh seemed to hang about him from the quickness he had been reduced in bulk by long marches, and anxiety of mind. He addressed a few words to the colonel in a firm and manly tone, and begged him to consider his situation and circumstances, and that he was the husband of a respectable woman, and father of several children; but, however, it was not possible for the colonel to forgive him at that time, and he was ordered to be quick and prepare. The farmer, accordingly, stripped, and was tied up. The colonel addressed him, and referred to the offer he had made him when in confinement, which, he told him, had much aggravated his crime, as supposing him (the colonel) capable of selling his honour for sixty pounds. So the farmer received his seven hundred lashes that day, and never uttered a word of complaint during the infliction, except that, as he sometimes turned his head, and looked after the can of water, he would say, 'Oh! poor Tom! poor Tom! I little thought ever to come to this!' I remember, after four hundred, the colonel asked him if he would sign his banishment, telling him it was to send him to another regiment, which was in foreign parts; but the farmer refused to do so, and the punishment went on. I recollect, too, that the doctor desired the drummer to lay the lash on the other shoulder, and the farmer received the whole sentence, as he well deserved. In a week or more he was to be seen walking in the barrack-square; but he avoided the society of the men, and in about two or three days afterwards, he was missing altogether, having taken an opportunity to escape; and we never again either heard of, or saw, the Yorkshire farmer.

There was another agriculturist who, I remember, was in the Rifles with me. He was the eldest son of a gentleman-farmer, who resided in Yorkshire, and as handsome a youth as I think I ever beheld; but he was one of the wildest chaps, perhaps, in the whole county, and, although he was not above four or five-and-twenty, his parents had found it out to their cost. In one of his sprees, happening to fall in with Sergeant Sugden of our corps, nothing would content him but he must enlist. Sugden, you may easily conceive, was not averse to indulge such a 'perspiring' hero, and very soon had him for a recruit. Although there must have been considerable difference in the style of life amongst us to what he had been used to, yet he appeared nowise displeased with the change. To be sure, he was rather too lively a bird at times, and, having plenty of money, occasionally got himself into trouble, but nothing particularly disagreeable happened, and altogether he was very much liked in the corps, in which he went by the name of 'The Gentleman Farmer.' Just before a detachment of the Rifles started for Portugal, a gentleman rode into the barrack-square, and inquired of some of the men for this young spark, whose name I cannot now remember. The meeting was not a very amicable one, for the newcomer was the gentleman-farmer's brother, who upbraided him with his conduct in enlisting, and told of the anxiety and sorrow this new freak had caused at home. After they had somewhat mollified their quarrel, they sought an interview with our commanding officer; and the brother immediately, in the name of the parents, offered any reasonable sum the colonel chose to name, so he would but grant the gentleman-farmer's discharge. The colonel, however, was not willing to lose him, and refused at that time to grant the request.

'He is a wild and untamed spirit,' he said; 'and as he is just now under orders for foreign service, he had better go; let him have a year of that fun; it will do his complaint good; and, if he lives, we shall see him, I hope, return an improved man.'

The new-comer, therefore, was fain to put up with this answer, and next morning returned home to his parents, apparently much cut up and disappointed at his ill-success. Accordingly the gentleman-farmer embarked for Portugal, and was soon after witness of a wilder scene of discord and horror than, I dare say, even his hair-brained ideas quite contemplated when he enlisted for a soldier; in short, he took his first lesson of actual warfare at the siege of Badajoz, and, entering with heart and soul into the breach, his head was dashed into a hundred pieces by a cannon ball.

Thomas Mayberry was a man well known at that time in the Rifles. He was a sergeant in my day, and was much thought of by our officers as a very active and useful non-commissioned officer, being considered, up to the time of his committing the slight mistake I shall have to tell of, one of the most honest men in the army. With the men he was not altogether so well liked, as he was considered rather too blusterous and tyrannical. Whilst in the town of Hythe, he got the fingering of about two hundred pounds for the purpose of paying for necessaries purchased for the men of his company, and which two hundred pounds he had, in a very short space of time, managed to make away with, and lose in the society of a party of gamblers, who at that time infested the town of Hythe. Captain Hart, who then commanded the company Mayberry belonged to, was not a little thunderstruck, some little time after, at finding that the several tradesmen who furnished the articles for the men had never been settled with, and, sending for Mayberry, discovered the delinquency. Mayberry was a prisoner in a moment; and Captain Hart was as much astonished as if his own father had committed a fraud, so well and so much was Mayberry thought of. He was brought to court-martial, together with two other men, whom he had seduced to become partners in his gambling transactions; and, on the inquiry, it was further discovered that he had been in the habit of cheating the men of his company out of a farthing a week each for the last ten months. That was, perhaps, the worst thing against him. He was sentenced to receive seven hundred lashes. Corporal Morrisson and Patrick Divine, his two participators in this roguery, got, I remember, the former three, and the latter one hundred, awarded to them.

When the square was formed for punishment, and the three were brought out, it was necessary to check the men of the regiment, or they would have hooted and hissed them on the parade. I recollect, also, that there was a civilian, of the name of Gilbert, whom Mayberry had defrauded, and he had inquired the time of his punishment, and was present in the rear during the infliction, having expressed to some of Mayberry's companions that he was content to lose the money, so that he saw the fellow well flogged – a pretty good proof that, when their own interests are nearly concerned, your civilian has no objection to even being an eye-witness of the infliction of the lash, about which there has lately been such an outcry. It is, indeed, no uncommon thing nowadays to see a man who has committed crimes, which have caused him to receive the execrations of his sometime companions in arms, as he is being drummed out of the corps, received by a host of folks without the barrack-gates, and taken to their bosoms as an object of commiseration.

When Mayberry was tied up, he was offered, as was then customary, the option of banishment; but he refused it, notwithstanding considerable entreaty was made to him by his two comrades to accept it, as, by so doing, they thought they all would escape the lash. However, Mayberry decided to take the seven hundred, and bore the sentence without a murmur. Not so the two others: Morrisson screamed and struggled so much that he capsized the triangle, and all came sprawling together, so that he was obliged to be held by a man at each side. Divine came last. He was rather an effeminate-looking man; and the colonel rode round, and told him he lamented being obliged to break so fair a skin; but he must do his duty. However, as he had borne a good character, and was not so much to blame as the other two, he let him down after five and twenty.

Mayberry after this was much scouted by his fellow-soldiers, and also ill-thought of by the officers; and, on a detachment being sent to Portugal, he volunteered for the expedition. Captain Hart, however, would fain have declined taking him, as he had so bad an opinion of him after this affair; but Mayberry showed himself so desirous of going, that at last he consented and took him. At the siege of Badajoz, Mayberry wiped off, in a measure, all his former ill-conduct. He was seen by Captain Hart to behave so bravely in the breach that he commended him on the spot.

'Well done, Mayberry!' said he; 'you have this day done enough to obliterate your disgrace; and, if we live, I will endeavour to restore you to your former rank. Go now to the rear; you have done enough for one day.' Mayberry, however, refused to retire, although covered with wounds; for he was known to have killed seven with his own hand with his rifle sword-bayonet.

'No going to the rear for me,' he said. 'I'll restore myself to my comrades' opinion, or make a finish of myself altogether.'

He accordingly continued in the front of all, till at last he was seen to be cut down, in the clear light of the fire-balls, by a tremendous sword-cut, which cleft his skull almost in twain. Morrisson, I heard, also died at that siege. Divine returned safe home, and died of fatigue at Fermoy.

It has been said, I have heard, by officers of high rank in the army of the Peninsula, that there never were such a set of devil-may-care fellows, and so completely up to their business, as the 95th. It would be invidious to make a distinction or talk of any one regiment being better, or more serviceable, than another; but the Rifles were generally in the mess before the others began, and also the last to leave off. It was their business to be so; and if they did their work well, so did every other British corps engaged in that country, at least I never either heard or saw to the contrary. There was, perhaps, as intelligent and talented a set of men amongst us, as ever carried a weapon in any country. They seemed at times to need but a glance at what was going on to know all about its 'why and wherefore.' I remember seeing the Duke of Wellington during the battle of Vimeiro; and in these days, when so much anxiety is displayed to catch even a glance of that great man's figure as he gallops along the streets of London, it seems gratifying to me to recollect seeing him in his proper element, 'the raging and bloody field,' and I have frequently taxed my mind to remember each action and look I caught of him at that time.

I remember seeing the great Duke take his hat off in the field of Vimeiro, and methinks it is something to have seen that wonderful man even do so commonplace a thing as lift his hat to another officer in the battle-field. We were generally enveloped in smoke and fire, and sometimes unable to distinguish or make remarks upon what was going on around, whilst we blazed away at our opponents; but occasionally we found time to make our comments upon the game we were playing. Two or three fellows near me were observing what was going on just in the rear, and I heard one man remark, 'Here comes Sir Arthur and his staff'; upon which I also looked back, and caught sight of him just meeting with two other officers of high rank. They all uncovered as they met, and I saw the Duke as I said (then Sir Arthur Wellesley) take off his hat and bow to the other two. The names of the new-comers, however they were learnt, whether from some of the men who had before seen them, or picked up on the instant from an officer, seemed to be well known, as well as the business they were engaged in talking of; for it ran along the line from one to the other that Sir Hew Dalrymple and Sir Harry Burrard were about to take the command, instead of Sir Arthur Wellesley, a circumstance which, of course, could only be a random guess amongst these fellows at the moment.*

The intelligence of these men was indeed very great, and I could relate instances of their recklessness and management which would amuse the reader much. I remember a fellow named Jackman getting close up to the walls at Flushing [during the Walcheren expedition of 1809], and working a hole in the earth with his sword, into which he laid himself, and remained there alone, spite of all the efforts of the enemy and their various missiles to dislodge him. He was known, thus earthed, to have killed, with the utmost coolness and deliberation, eleven of the French artillerymen, as they worked at their guns. As fast as they relieved each fallen comrade did Jackman pick them off; after which he took to his heels, and got safe back to his comrades.

* Although the Secretary at War, Lord Castlereagh, had wanted Wellesley to command the expedition, the objections of other members of the Government and of the senior officers of the Horse Guards to the appointment of so young and vaguely suspect a sepoy general had led to the command being given to the much older Sir Hew Dalrymple (1750–1830), the Governor of Gibraltar. Sir Harry Burrard (1755–1813), also a veteran Guards Officer, was appointed second-in-command.

There were three brothers in the Rifles named Hart – John, Mike, and Peter – and three more perfectly reckless fellows, perhaps, never existed. Nothing ever escaped their notice; and they would create the greatest fun and laughter, even when advancing under the hottest fire of the enemy, and their comrades being shot down beside them. I remember Lieutenant Molloy, who was himself as fine a 'soldier as ever stepped, and as full of life in the midst of death' as these Harts, being obliged to check them at Vimeiro. 'D—n you!' he said to them, 'keep back, and get under cover. Do you think you are fighting here with your fists, that you are running into the teeth of the French?'

I never saw those three men, to appearance, the least worse for hard work during the time we remained in Portugal. They could run like deer, and were indeed formed by Nature and disposition for the hardships, difficulties, and privations of the sort of life we then led. They were, however, all three pretty well done up during the retreat to Coruña; though, even in that dreadful business, their light-heartedness and attempts at fun served to keep up the spirits of many a man who would else have been broken-hearted before the English shipping appeared in sight. They even carried their pleasantry on that occasion so far as to make a jest of their own appearance, and the miserable plight of the whole turn-out, as we disembarked upon the beach at Portsmouth. One of them even went so far as to observe, 'that we looked more like the rakings of h— than the fragments of an army!'

Nothing, indeed, but that grave of battalions, that unwholesome fen, Flushing, could have broken the spirits of three such soldiers as John, Mike, and Peter Hart. A few weeks, however, of that country sufficed to quiet them for evermore. One, I remember, died; and the other two, although they lived to return, were never worth a rush afterwards, but, like myself, remained living examples of what climate can bring even a constitution and body framed as if of iron to.

Nothing, I suppose, could exceed the dreadful appearance we cut on the occasion of the disembarkation from Coruña; and the inhabitants of Portsmouth, who had assembled in some numbers to see us land, were horror-stricken with the sight of their countrymen and relatives returning to England in such a ghastly state; whilst the three Harts, with feet swathed in bloody rags, clothing that hardly covered their nakedness, accoutrements in shreds, beards covering their faces, eyes dimmed with toil (for some were even blind), arms nearly useless to those who had them left, the rifles being encrusted with rust, and the swords glued to the scabbard; these three brothers, I say (for I heard them myself), as they hobbled up the beach, were making all sorts of remarks, and cracking their jokes upon the misery of our situation, and the appearance they themselves cut.

I recollect seeing at this time an affecting instance of female affection displayed. One of our officers, whose name I will not mention, and who was much beloved by us all, observed his wife waiting for him on the beach, as he disembarked from the boat. He met her as she rushed into the sea to embrace him, and they were locked in each others' arms before they touched the dry land.

9

WHILST we lay near Cork we were joined by one Richard
Pullen, amongst others; he had exchanged from the English
militia into the Irish, and volunteered to us Rifles from the
North Mayo. He brought with him little else to boast of but
his wife and his two children, Charles and Susan. Charles
was a mischievous boy of about twelve, and Susan was a
pretty little lass, of about fourteen years of age. I remember
they all went with us to Copenhagen, and got through that
expedition pretty well. That affair suited a man of Pullen's
description, for he didn't like too much service; and we soon
found he was rather a shy cock. 'None of your North Mayho
here, Master Pullen!' used to be constantly flung in his teeth,
when he was lagging behind on the march. In 1808 he was
again wanted, when our four companies went to Portugal;
but Pullen begged off, on account of the wife and the two
children, Charles and Susan. Often had he to endure the
taunt again, 'None of your North Mayho here, Master
Pullen!' till we were fairly away from Hythe.

After we had knocked the frogs out of Portugal, marching
on Sahagun, we fell in with the army under Sir John Moore,*
and, amongst the Rifles that came with them fresh from
England, we found Pullen and his wife, with their two chil-

* By the terms of the Convention of Cintra (August 1808), the
French had withdrawn their troops from Portugal. On 25th Sep-
tember, Sir John Moore (1761–1809) was instructed by Lord
Castlereagh to assume command of a force of 35,000 men which
was 'to co-operate with the Spanish armies in the expulsion of
the French from Spain'.

dren, Charles and Susan. I remember that the meeting with Pullen caused no small fun amongst us; and North Mayho was again the bye-word for a few days. Nothing, I thought at that time, could tame down the high spirits and thoughtlessness of the British soldier. Alas! I lived to see that I was mistaken; and, indeed, saw them pretty well tamed before many days more were over our heads! I remember remarking that Pullen (even on the first day of the retreat to Coruña) looked very chapfallen and seedy; and he was beginning even then to complain that he could not stand much more. The wife and children, too, were dropping behind. *They* all thought, poor souls! that when night came on they were, of course, to be billeted; but the open world was now their only refuge; and no allowance to stop or lie down, even on the bare heath, at that time. I saw Pullen again on the third or fourth day; neither the wife nor children were then with him, nor could he tell *where* they were; he could only answer for himself, and expected to drop dead, he said, every step. That's all I saw of Pullen, and his wife and children, on the retreat, or even thought of them; for I had enough to do to keep my own strength up. When we landed at Portsmouth, both myself and others (to our no small surprise) saw Pullen once more; and much we wondered at the sight of him, when so many better and stronger soldiers had died before half of that retreat was accomplished. We had not even then spirits enough left to jeer him about North Mayho; and, to add to the dejection of poor Pullen, we found that he had left behind him, and knew nothing of the fate of either his wife or his children, Charles and Susan. As the men continued to disembark, however, there was Pullen inquiring anxiously of every one for some tidings of them. None, however, could he get. At last he saw his wife coming up the beach, and hobbled off to meet her, each at the same moment inquiring for the children, Charles and Susan. *He* trusted they were with the wife; and *she* hoped they were with the husband; and both sat down upon the beach, and cried in concert. All our men thought it useless of them to continue their inquiries; but they never failed to ask after their offspring of every fresh face they fell in with, who had been in that retreat. In about a fortnight's time, not satisfied, they advertised Charles and Susan in the public newspapers; and we all laughed at the very idea of their ever finding them again, and told them they might have spared the money. To our no small surprise, however, the artillery at Plymouth answered their advertisement, stating that a little girl had been heard screaming upon the mountains in Spain by them in the night, and that they had taken care of her as well as they could, and had her then with them. The description answering, the girl was forwarded to Hythe; and Pullen and his wife once more embraced their daughter Susan.

Meanwhile, no tidings came of the boy; and Pullen died at Walcheren, with many a gallant soldier for his fellow-victim in that dreadful country. The wife had confessed long before that the child she had given birth to after the retreat, she had every reason to believe, was a Frenchman by the father's side; for she related her adventures to many of us at that time, and told, amongst other things, that she and other women, having taken refuge in a barn, were there overtaken by the French in the night, and treated by those gentlemen in a very unceremonious manner.

It is easy to suppose that Mrs Pullen had no great wish to go on service again, and much did she endeavour to persuade Pullen to evade it too; but, the whole regiment being under orders for Walcheren, Pullen could not escape the chance. At last, however, he tried to excuse himself by tampering with his eyes, which he made sore by putting snuff in them. He was, however, detected, disgraced, and, sailing with the expedition, died, as I before said, at Walcheren.

After his death, Mrs Pullen and her daughter were sent to their parish, which was in Warwickshire; and, after she had left us some time, a letter arrived from her son, Charles, who was a prisoner in France. There was, I think, not a man in the regiment who recollected the North Mayho recruit but myself. War, and pestilence, and discharge, had taken all away. The bugle-major opened the letter; and, on inquiry, found that I alone knew the parents of the writer; but no answer, that I ever heard of, was sent to poor Charles. The captain of Pullen's company (Crampton) was dead, and the company was almost entirely new. I myself was then almost in a dying state, and the matter was soon altogether forgotten. So that, whether Mrs Pullen ever again saw her son, I cannot take upon me to say.

CHANCES OF WARFARE

It was during the heat of the day of Vimeiro. We were rather hotly pressed by the enemy after having advanced somewhat too near their force. Give and take is all fair enough; but we were getting more kicks than halfpence, as the saying is; and their balls stung us so sharply that the officers gave the word to 'fire and retire.' Doubtless, many got a leaden messenger as they did so, which saved them the unpleasant necessity of retracing their ground altogether. Jock Gillespie and myself wheeled about, and obeyed the order. Just as we had done so, I saw Gillespie limp along as though some one had bestowed a violent kick upon his person. However, he didn't give up at first, but continued to load, and fire, and make off with the other skirmishers, till we halted, and made another stand; for we never went further from them when once engaged, than we could possibly help.

Gillespie loaded, and fired very sharply, I recollect, seemingly quite affronted at the treatment he had received; but he got weaker and more lame as he did so, and at last was quite unable to continue the game any longer; and, when we advanced again, he was floored from loss of blood. I had asked him once or twice where he was hit, but he seemed unwilling to say, till at last he confessed; and the confession gave him apparently as much pain as the wound.

After the battle was over, I observed him endeavouring to get about, and limping as badly as if one leg was a foot shorter than the other, whilst our men, who had got hold of the story kept calling after, and making all sorts of fun about his wound; till poor Gillespie (who was a very sensitive man) sat down and cried like a child with vexation. I never saw him

65

after that night; and I rather think his wound had completely disabled him, and that eventually he got a discharge.

I remember a great many of the leaders and heroes of the wars of my own time. Alas! they have been cleared off of late pretty handsomely! A few years more, and the world will be without another living remembrancer of either them or their deeds. The ranks are getting thin, too, amongst those who, like myself, were the tools with which the great men of former days won their renown. I don't know a single living man now who was a comrade during the time I served. Very nearly fifteen years back, I remember, however, meeting with Robert Liston; and that meeting brings Marshal Beresford* to my mind. Robert Liston was a corporal in the second battalion of the Rifles, when we lay for a few days in the passages of a convent in Portugal. We were then making for the frontiers of Spain, when we were swept into that disastrous retreat to Coruña. There was a punishment parade in the square of this convent. A soldier of the 92nd or 79th was the culprit, and the kilts were formed to witness the performance. Some of the Rifles were looking from the windows of the convent at the punishment of the Highlander, when a brickbat was hurled from one of the casements, and fell at the very toe of the lieutenant-colonel, who was standing in the midst, and in command of the regiment. The lieutenant-colonel (whose name I never knew) was of course indignant at such an act; he gazed up at the window from which the brick had been thrown, and caused an inquiry instantly to be made. It was between the lights when this happened, and it was impossible to discover who had done it; however, two or three men of the Rifles were confined on suspicion. A man named Baker flatly accused Corporal Liston of the act; upon which Liston was marched a prisoner to Salamanca (a distance, I should think, of some hundred miles); and often did he com-

* Major-General William Carr Beresford (1768–1854). He became a Marshal in the Portuguese Army in 1809 on his appointment to the command of a military mission whose help in the reform of their disorganized forces had been requested by the Portuguese government.

plain of his hard fate in being a prisoner so long. When we got to Salamanca we halted there for eight days; and Liston, being tried by general court-martial, was sentenced to receive eight hundred lashes. The whole brigade turned out on the occasion; and I remember that the drummers of the 9th regiment were the inflictors of the lash. Liston received the whole sentence without a murmur. He had, indeed, been a good soldier, and we were all truly sorry for him; in fact, he always declared solemnly that he had no more to do with the brickbat than Marshal Beresford who commanded the brigade. Whoever committed the act, in my opinion, well deserved what *Liston got*. Marshal Beresford was in command of the brigade at this time; and I well remember what a fine-looking soldier he was. He was equal to his business, too, I should say; and he, amongst others of our generals, often made me think that the French army had nothing to show in the shape of officers who could at all compare with ours. There was a noble bearing in our leaders, which they, on the French side (as far as I was capable of observing) had not; and I am convinced that the English soldier is even better pleased to be commanded by some man of rank in his own country, than by one who has risen from his own station.

They are a strange set, the English! and so determined and unconquerable, that they will have their way if they can. Indeed, it requires one who has authority in his face, as well as at his back, to make them respect and obey him. They see too often, in the instance of sergeant-majors, that command does not suit ignorant and coarse-minded men; and that tyranny is too much used even in the brief authority which they have. A soldier, I am convinced, is driven often to insubordination by being worried by these little-minded men for the veriest trifles, about which the gentleman never thinks of tormenting him. The moment the severity of the discipline of our army is relaxed, in my opinion, farewell to its efficiency; but for our men to be tormented about trifles (as I have seen at times) is often very injurious to a whole corps.

I never saw Liston after that punishment whilst in Spain; and I suppose he remained behind, and got on in the best manner he was able in the rear; but, about ten years afterwards, as I was passing down Sloane Street, Chelsea, I observed a watchman calling the hour. It struck me that I knew his face, and, turning back, I stopped him, asking if he was not Robert Liston, formerly a corporal in the 95th Rifles? After answering in the affirmative, the first words he spoke were, 'Oh! Harris! do you remember what happened to me at Salamanca?'

'I do well,' I said.

'I was never guilty,' he continued. 'There is no occasion for me to deny it now; but I tell you that I was never guilty of the crime for which I suffered. Baker was a villain, and I believe that he was himself the culprit.'

I recollect Marshal Beresford making a speech on the subject of the buttons of our great-coats; and, however such a subject may appear trifling for a general officer to speak on, I can tell you, it was a discourse which our men (some of them) much needed; for they had been in the habit of tearing off the buttons from their coats, and after hammering them flat, passing them as English coin, in exchange for the good wines of Spain. So that, at last, the Spaniards, finding they got nothing by the exchange but trumpery bits of battered lead, and the children in that country not being in the habit of playing at dumps as ours are, they made complaints to the marshal. Halting the brigade, therefore, one day, he gave them a speech upon this fraud, and ended by promising a handsome flogging to the first man he found thereafter whose great-coat would not keep buttoned in windy weather.

10

A T Sahagun we fell in with the army under command of Sir
John Moore. I forget how many thousand men there were;
but they were lying in and around the town when we
arrived.* The Rifles marched to an old convent, some two
miles from Sahagun, where we were quartered, together with
a part of the 15th Hussars, some of the Welsh fusileers and
straggling bodies of men belonging to various other regiments; all seeming on the *qui vive*, and expecting the French
to fall in with them every hour. As our small and way-worn
party came to a halt before the walls of the convent, the men
from these different regiments came swarming out to greet
us, loudly cheering us as they rushed up and seized our
hands. The difference in appearance between ourselves and
these new-comers was indeed (just then) very great. *They*
looked fresh, from good quarters, and good rations. Their
clothes and accoutrements were comparatively new and
clean, and their cheeks ruddy with the glow of health and
strength; whilst our men, on the contrary, were gaunt-look-

* Moore had advanced from Salamanca on 11 December, 1808,
and arrived at Sahagun towards the end of the month, throwing
his army across the French communications. But having drawn off
Napoleon's army from Madrid, he found himself so outnumbered
and his own communications so seriously threatened by the
Emperor's quick reaction that, with no hope of assistance from
the ineffectual Spanish armies, he decided to withdraw to the
coast.

ing, way-worn, and ragged; our faces burnt almost to the hue of an Asiatic's by the sun; our accoutrements rent and torn; and many without even shoes to their feet. However, we had some work in us yet; and perhaps were in better condition for it than our more fresh-looking comrades. And now our butchers tucked up their sleeves, and quickly set to work, slaughtering oxen and sheep, which we found within the convent walls; whilst others of our men, lighting fires in the open air upon the snow, commenced cooking the fragments, which were cut up, and distributing to them; so that very soon after our arrival, we were more sumptuously regaled than we had been for many days.

After this meal we were ordered into the convent and, with knapsacks on our backs, and arms in our hands, threw ourselves down to rest upon the floor of a long passage. Overcome with hard toil and long miles, our wearied men were soon buried in a deep and heavy sleep. In the middle of the night I remember, as well as if the sounds were at this moment in my ear, that my name was called out many times without my being completely awakened by the summons. The repeated call seemed mixed up with some circumstance in my dreams; and it was not until the noise awoke some of the men lying nearer to the entrance of the passage, and they took up the cry, that I was effectually aroused. From weariness, and the weight of my knapsack, and the quantity of implements I carried, I was at first quite unable to gain my legs; but when I did so I found that Quartermaster Surtees* was the person who was thus disturbing my rest.

'Come, be quick there, Harris!' said he, as I picked my way by the light of the candle he held in his hand; 'look amongst the men, and rouse up all the shoemakers you have in the four companies. I have a job for them, which must be done instantly.'

With some little trouble, and not a few curses from them as I stirred them up with the butt of my rifle, I succeeded in

* William Surtees, the author of *Twenty-Five Years in The Rifle Brigade* (1833).

70

waking several of our snoring handicrafts; and the quarter-master bidding us instantly follow him, led the way to the very top of the convent stairs. Passing then into a ruinous-looking apartment, along which we walked upon the rafters, there being no flooring, he stopped when he arrived at its further extremity. Here he proceeded to call our attention to a quantity of barrels of gunpowder lying beside a large heap of raw bullocks' hides.

'Now, Harris,' said he, 'keep your eyes open, and mind what you are about here. General Craufurd orders you instantly to set to work, and sew up every one of these barrels in the hides lying before you. You are to sew the skins with the hair outwards, and be quick about it, for the general swears that if the job is not finished in half an hour he will hang you.'

The latter part of this order was anything but pleasant; and whether the general ever really gave it I never had an opportunity of ascertaining. I only know that I give the words as they were given me; and, well knowing the stuff Craufurd was made of, I received the candle from the hands of Surtees, and bidding the men get needles and waxed thread from their knapsacks, as the quartermaster withdrew, I instantly prepared to set about the job.

I often think of that night's work as I sit strapping away in my little shop in Richmond Street, Soho. It was a curious scene to look at, and the task neither very easy nor safe. The Riflemen were wearied, unwilling, and out of temper; and it was as much as I could do to get them to assist me. Moreover, they were so reckless that they seemed rather to wish to blow the convent into the air than to get on with their work. One moment the candle was dropped, and nearly extinguished; the next they lost their implements between the rafters of the floor, flaring the light about amongst the barrels; and wishing, as I remonstrated with them, that the powder might ignite, and blow me, themselves, and the general to——. Such were the Riflemen of the Peninsula War—daring, gallant, reckless fellows. I had a hard task to get the work safely finished; but at length, between coaxing and

71

bullying these dare-devils, I managed to do so, and together we returned down the convent stairs; and, finding Surtees awaiting us in the passage below, he reported to General Craufurd that his order had been obeyed. After which we were permitted again to lie down, and sleep till the bugle awoke us next morning.

We remained in the convent part of the next day, and towards evening received orders to leave all our women and baggage behind, and advance towards the enemy. Our four companies accordingly were quickly upon the move, and before long we came up with the remainder of the Rifle corps, which had recently arrived from England with Sir John Moore. As these men saw us coming up they halted for the moment, and gave us one hearty cheer, allowing our four companies to pass to the front, as the post of honour, calling us 'The heroes of Portugal.' As we passed to the front we returned their cheer with pride. Our worn appearance and sunburnt look gave us the advantage over our comrades, we thought, and we marched in the van of the vanguard.

War is a sad blunter of the feelings of men. We felt eager to be at it again. Nay, I am afraid we longed for blood as the cheer of our comrades sounded in our ears; and yet, amidst all this, softer feelings occasionally filled the breasts of those gallant fellows, even whilst they were thirsting for a sight of the enemy. Some of the men near me suddenly recollected, as they saw the snow lying thickly in our path, that this was Christmas Eve. The recollection soon spread amongst the men; and many talked of home, and scenes upon that night in other days in Old England, shedding tears as they spoke of the relatives and friends never to be seen by them again.

As the night approached we became less talkative. The increasing weariness of our limbs kept our tongues quieter, and we were many of us half asleep as we walked, when suddenly a shout arose in front that the French were upon us. In an instant every man was on the alert, and we were rushing forward, in extended order, to oppose them. It proved a false alarm, but it nearly cost me a broken bone or two.

The honourable Captain Pakenham (now Sir Hercules Pakenham), on the first sound of the enemy being in sight, made a dash to get to the front, at the same moment I myself was scrambling up a bank on the road side. In the darkness and hurry the mule the captain was mounted on bore me to the ground, and, getting his fore-feet fast fixed somehow between my neck and my pack, we were fairly hampered for some moments. The captain swore, the mule floundered, and I bellowed with alarm lest the animal should dig his feet into my back, and quite disable me. At length, however, the captain succeeded in getting clear, and spurred over the bank, as I rolled back into the road. It might be somewhere about two o'clock in the morning that our advance into Spain was, for that time, checked, and the retreat to Coruña might be said to commence. General Craufurd was in command of the brigade, and riding in front, when I observed a dragoon come spurring furiously along the road to meet us. He delivered a letter to the general, who turned round in his saddle the moment he had read a few lines, and thundered out the word 'to halt!' A few minutes more and we were all turned to the right-about and retracing our steps of the night before – the contents of that epistle serving to furnish our men with many a surmise during the retrograde movement. When we again neared Sahagun, I remember seeing the wives and children of the men come rushing into the ranks, and embracing the husbands and fathers they expected never to see again.

The entire Rifle corps entered the same convent we had before been quartered in; but this time we remained enranked in its apartments and passages, no man being allowed to quit his arms or lie down. We stood leaning upon the muzzles of our rifles, and dozed as we stood. After remaining thus for about an hour, we were then ordered out of the convent, and the word was again given to march. There was a sort of thaw on this day, and the rain fell fast. As we passed the walls of the convent, I observed our General (Craufurd) as he sat upon his horse, looking at us on the march, and remarked the peculiar sternness of his features: he did not

73

like to see us going rearwards at all; and many of us judged there must be something wrong by his severe look and scowling eye.

'Keep your ranks there, men!' he said, spurring his horse towards some Riflemen who were avoiding a small rivulet. 'Keep your ranks and move on – *no straggling* from the main body.'

We pushed on all that day without halting; and I recollect the first thing that struck us as somewhat odd was our passing one of the commissariat wagons, overturned and stuck fast in the mud, and which was abandoned without an effort to save any of its contents. A sergeant of the 92nd Highlanders, just about this time, fell dead with fatigue, and no one stopped, as we passed, to offer him any assistance. Night came down upon us, without our having tasted food, or halted – I speak for myself, and those around me – and all night long we continued this dreadful march. Men began to look into each other's faces, and ask the question, 'Are we ever to be halted again?' and many of the weaker sort were now seen to stagger, make a few desperate efforts, and then fall, perhaps to rise no more. Most of us had devoured all we carried in our haversacks, and endeavoured to catch up anything we could snatch from hut or cottage in our route. Many, even at this period, would have straggled from the ranks, and perished, had not Craufurd held them together with a firm rein. One such bold and stern commander in the East during a memorable disaster, and that devoted army had reached its refuge unbroken! Thus we staggered on, night and day, for about four days, before we discovered the reason of this continued forced march. The discovery was made to our company by a good-tempered, jolly fellow, named Patrick M'Lauchlan. He inquired of an officer, marching directly in his front, the destination intended.

'By J—s! Musther Hills,' I heard him say, 'where the d—l is this you're taking us to?'

'To England, M'Lauchlan,' returned the officer with a melancholy smile upon his face as he gave the answer – '*if we can get there.*'

74

'More luck and grace to you,' said M'Lauchlan; 'and it's that you're maning, is it?'

This M'Lauchlan was a good specimen of a thorough Irish soldier. Nothing could disturb his good humour and high spirits; and even during a part of this dreadful march, he had ever some piece of Irish humour upon his tongue's end, whilst he staggered under the weight of his pack. He would in all probability have been amongst the few who did reach England; but, during the march, he was attacked with the racking pains of acute rheumatism, and frequently fell to the ground screaming with agony. On such occasions his companions would do that for him which they omitted to perform towards others. They many times halted, heaved him up, and assisted him forwards. Sir Dudley Hill,* too, was greatly interested for M'Lauchlan, trying to cheer him on, whilst the men could scarcely refrain from laughter at the extraordinary things he gave utterance to whilst racked with pain, and staggering with fatigue. At length, however, M'Lauchlan fell one dark night, as we hurried through the streets of a village, and we could not again raise him.

'It's no use, Harris,' I heard him say in a faint voice, 'I can do no more.'

Next morning, when day broke, he was no longer seen in the ranks, and as I never saw him again I conclude he quickly perished.

* Dudley St. Leger Hill (1790–1851). At this time a junior officer in the 95th, he was knighted in 1816 while serving with the Portuguese Army and promoted Major-General in 1841. At the time of his death he was commanding a division in Bengal.

11

THE information M'Lauchlan obtained from Lieutenant Hill quickly spread amongst us, and we now began to see more clearly the horrors of our situation, and the men to murmur at not being permitted to turn and stand at bay – cursing the French, and swearing they would rather die ten thousand deaths, with their rifles in their hands in opposition, than endure the present toil. We were in the rear at this time, and following that part of the army which made for Vigo,* whilst the other portion of the British, being on the main road to Coruña, were at this moment closely pursued and harassed by the enemy, as I should judge from the continued thunder of their cannon and rattle of their musketry. Craufurd seemed to sniff the sound of battle from afar with peculiar feelings. He halted us for a few minutes occasionally when the distant clamour became more distinct, and his face turned towards the sound and seemed to light up and become less stern. It was then indeed that every poor fellow clutched his weapon more firmly, and wished for a sight of the enemy.

Before long they had their wish: the enemy's cavalry

* Harris's Battalion left Sahagun on Christmas Day 1808 and arrived at Astorga on the 31st. At Astorga the light brigades were detached from the main body and, in order to keep the main army safe from attack on its southern flank and to lessen the strain on the resources of the Commissariat, they were sent through Ponferrada and Orense to Vigo.

were on our skirts that night; and as we rushed out of a small village, the name of which I cannot now recollect, we turned to bay.* Behind broken-down carts and tumbrils, huge trunks of trees, and everything we could scrape together, the Rifles lay and blazed away at the advancing cavalry, whilst the inhabitants, suddenly aroused from their beds to behold their village almost on fire with our continued discharges, and nearly distracted with the sound, ran from their houses, crying 'Viva l'Englisa!' and 'Viva la Franca!' in a breath; men, women, and children flying to the open country in their alarm.

We passed the night thus engaged, holding our own as well as we could, together with the 43rd Light Infantry, the 52nd, a portion of the German Legion, part of the 10th Hussars, and the 15th Dragoons. Towards morning we moved down towards a small bridge, still followed by the enemy, whom, however, we had sharply galled, and obliged to be more wary in their efforts. The rain was pouring down in torrents on this morning I recollect, and we remained many hours with our arms ported, standing in this manner, and staring the French cavalry in the face, the water actually running out of the muzzles of our rifles. I do not recollect seeing a single regiment of infantry amongst the French force on this day; it seemed to me a tremendous body of cavalry – some said nine or ten thousand strong – commanded, as I heard, by General Lefebvre.†

Whilst we stood thus, face to face, I remember the horsemen of the enemy sat watching us very intently, as if waiting for a favourable moment to dash upon us like beasts of prey; and every now and then their trumpets would ring out a lively strain of music, as if to encourage them. As the night drew on, our cavalry moved a little to the front, together with several field-pieces, and succeeded in crossing the bridge; after which we also advanced, and threw ourselves into some hilly ground on either side the road; whilst the 43rd and 52nd

* This was at Castro Gonzalo.

† General Comte Charles Lefebvre-Desnouëttes (1773–1822). He was later captured at Benavente.

lay behind some carts, trunks of trees, and other materials with which they had formed a barrier.

General Craufurd was standing behind this barricade, when he ordered the Rifles to push still further in front, and conceal themselves amongst the hills on either side. A man named Higgins was my front-rank man at this moment. 'Harris,' said he, 'let you and I gain the very top of the mountain, and look out what those French thieves are at on the other side.'

My feet were sore and bleeding, and the sinews of my legs ached as if they would burst, but I resolved to accompany him. In our wearied state the task was not easy, but, by the aid of Higgins, a tall and powerful fellow, I managed to reach the top of the mountain, where we placed ourselves in a sort of gully, or ditch, and looked over to the enemy's side, concealing ourselves by lying flat in the ditch, as we did so. Thus, in favourable situations, like cats watching for their prey, were the rest of the Rifles lying *perdu* upon the hills that night. The mountain, we found, was neither so steep nor so precipitous on the enemy's side. The ascent, on the contrary, was so easy, that one or two of the videttes of the French cavalry were prowling about very near where we lay. As we had received orders not to make more noise than we could help, not even to speak to each other except in whispers, although one of these horsemen approached close to where I lay, I forbore to fire upon him. At length he stopped so near me that I saw it was almost impossible he could avoid discovering that the Rifles were in such close proximity to his person. He gazed cautiously along the ridge, took off his helmet, and wiped his face, as he appeared to meditate upon the propriety of crossing the ditch in which we lay; when suddenly our eyes met, and in an instant he plucked a pistol from his holster, fired it in my face, and, wheeling his horse, plunged down the hillside. For the moment I thought I was hit, as the ball grazed my neck, and stuck fast in my knapsack, where I found it, when, many days afterwards, I unpacked my kit on ship-board. About a quarter of an hour after this, as we still lay in the gully, I heard some person clambering up behind us, and, upon turning quickly round, I found it was General Craufurd. The general was wrapped in his great-coat, and, like ourselves, had been for many hours drenched to the skin, for the rain was coming down furiously. He carried in his hand a canteen full of rum, and a small cup, with which he was occasionally endeavouring to refresh some of the men. He offered me a drink as he passed, and then proceeded onwards along the ridge. After he had emptied his canteen he came past us again, and himself gave us instructions as to our future proceedings.

'When all is ready, Riflemen,' said he, 'you will immediately get the word, and pass over the bridge. Be careful, and mind what you are about.'

Accordingly, a short time after he had left us, we were ordered to descend the mountain-side in single file, and having gained the road, were quickly upon the bridge. Meanwhile the Staff Corps had been hard at work mining the very centre of the structure, which was filled with gunpowder, a narrow plank being all the aid we had by which to pass over. For my own part, I was now so utterly helpless that I felt as if all was nearly up with me, and that, if I could steady myself so as to reach the further end of the plank, it would be all I should be able to accomplish. However, we managed all of us to reach the other side in safety, when, almost immediately afterwards, the bridge blew up with a tremendous report, and a house at its extremity burst into flames. What with the concussion of the explosion, and the tremulous state of my limbs, I was thrown to the ground, and lay flat upon my face for some time, almost in a state of insensibility. After awhile I somewhat recovered; but it was not without extreme difficulty, and many times falling again, that I succeeded in regaining the column. Soon after I had done so, we reached Benevento [Benavente], and immediately took refuge in a convent. Already three parts of it were filled with other troops, among which were mingled the 10th Hussars, the German Legion, and the 15th Dragoons; the horses of these regiments standing as close as they could stand, with the men dismounted between each horse, the animals' heads to the walls of the building, and all in readiness to turn out on the instant. Liquor was handed to us by the Dragoons, but having had nothing for some time to eat, many of our men became sick, instead of receiving any benefit from it.

Before we had been in the convent as long a time as I have been describing our arrival, every man of us was down on the floor, and wellnigh asleep; and before we had slept half an hour, we were again aroused from our slumbers by the clatter of the horses, the clash of the men's sabres, and their shouts for us to clear the way.

'The enemy! The enemy!' I heard shouted out.

'Clear the way, Rifles! Up boys, and clear the way!'

In short, the Dragoons hardly gave us time to rise, before they were leading their horses amongst us, and getting out of the convent as fast as they could scamper, whilst we ourselves were not long in following their example. As we did so, we discovered that the French cavalry, having found the bridge blown up, had dashed into the stream, and succeeded in crossing. Our cavalry, however, quickly formed, and charged them in gallant style.

The shock of that encounter was tremendous to look upon, and we stood for some time enranked, watching the combatants. The horsemen had it all to themselves; our Dragoons fought like tigers, and, although greatly overmatched, drove the enemy back like a torrent, and forced them again into the river. A private of the 10th Hussars—his name, I think, was Franklin—dashed into the stream after their general (Lefebvre), assailed him, sword in hand, in the water, captured, and brought him a prisoner on shore again. If I remember rightly, Franklin, or whatever else was his name, was made a sergeant on the spot.* The French general was delivered into our custody on that occasion, and we cheered the 10th men heartily as we received him.

After the enemy had received this check from our cavalry,

* Lefebvre-Desnouëttes was originally captured by a trooper of the King's German Legion who, not realizing the value of his prize, allowed the man from the 10th Hussars to lead him off the field.

and which considerably damped their ardour, making them a trifle more shy of us for a while, we pushed onwards on our painful march. I remember marching close beside the French general during some part of this day, and observing his chap-fallen and dejected look as he rode along in the midst of the green-jackets.

Being constantly in rear of the main body, the scenes of distress and misery I witnessed were dreadful to contemplate, particularly amongst the women and children, who were lagging and falling behind, their husbands and fathers being in the main body in our front. We now came to the edge of a deep ravine, the descent so steep and precipitous, that it was impossible to keep our feet in getting down, and we were sometimes obliged to sit and slide along on our backs; whilst before us rose a ridge of mountains quite as steep and difficult of ascent. There was, however, no pause in our exertion, but, slinging our rifles round our necks, down the hill we went; whilst mules with the baggage on their backs, wearied and urged beyond their strength, were seen rolling from top to bottom, many of them breaking their necks with the fall, and the baggage crushed, smashed, and abandoned.

I remember, as I descended this hill, remarking the extra-ordinary sight afforded by the thousands of our red-coats, who were creeping like snails, and toiling up the ascent before us, their muskets slung round their necks, and clam-bering with both hands as they hauled themselves up. As soon as we ourselves had gained the ascent we were halted for a few minutes, in order to give us breath for another effort, and then onwards we moved again.

It is impossible for me to keep any account of time in this description, as I never exactly knew how many days and nights we marched; but I well know we kept on for many successive days and nights, without rest, or much in the way of food. The long day found us still pushing on, and the night caused us no halt.

After leaving the hills I have mentioned, and which I heard at the time were called the Mountains of Galicia, as we passed through a village our major resolved to try and get

81

us something in the shape of a better meal than we had been able hitherto to procure. He accordingly despatched a small party, who were somewhat more fresh than their comrades, to try and procure something from the houses around; and they accordingly purchased, shot, and bayoneted somewhere about a score of pigs, which we lugged along with us to a convent just without the town; and, halting for a short time, proceeded to cook them. The men, however, were too hungry to wait whilst they were being properly dressed and served out.

After this hasty meal we again pushed on, still cursing the enemy for not again showing themselves, that we might revenge some of our present miseries upon their heads.

'Why don't they come on like men,' they cried, 'whilst we've strength left in us to fight them?'

We were now upon the mountains; the night was bitter cold, and the snow falling fast. As day broke, I remember hearing Lieutenant Hill say to another officer (who, by the way, afterwards sank down and died):

'This is New Year's Day; and I think if we live to see another we shall not easily forget it.'

The mountains were now becoming more wild-looking and steep as we proceeded; whilst those few huts we occasionally passed seemed so utterly forlorn and wretched-looking, it appeared quite a wonder how human beings could live in so desolate a home. After the snow commenced, the hills became so slippery (being in many parts covered with ice), that several of our men frequently slipped and fell, and being unable to rise, gave themselves up to despair, and died. There was now no endeavour to assist one another after a fall; it was everyone for himself, and God for us all!

The enemy, I should think, were at this time frequently close upon our trail; and I thought at times I heard their trumpets come down the wind as we marched. Towards the dusk of the evening of this day I remember passing a man and woman lying clasped in each other's arms, and dying in the snow. I knew them both; but it was impossible to help them.

They belonged to the Rifles, and were man and wife. The man's name was Joseph Sitdown. During this retreat, as he had not been in good health previously, himself and wife had been allowed to get on in the best way they could in the front. They had, however, now given in, and the last we ever saw of poor Sitdown and his wife was on that night lying perishing in each other's arms in the snow.

12

MANY trivial things which happened during the retreat to Coruña, and which on any other occasion might have entirely passed from my memory, have been, as it were, branded into my remembrance, and I recollect the most trifling incidents which occurred from day to day during that march. I remember, amongst other matters, that we were joined, if I may so term it, by a young recruit, when such an addition was anything but wished for during the disasters of the hour. One of the men's wives (who was struggling forward in the ranks with us, presenting a ghastly picture of illness, misery, and fatigue), being very large in the family-way, towards evening stepped from amongst the crowd, and lay herself down amidst the snow, a little out of the main road. Her husband remained with her; and I heard one or two hasty observations amongst our men that they had taken possession of their last resting-place. The enemy were, indeed, not far behind at this time, the night was coming down, and their chance seemed in truth but a bad one. To remain behind the column of march in such weather was to perish, and we accordingly soon forgot all about them. To my surprise, however, I, some little time afterwards (being myself then in the rear of our party), again saw the woman. She was hurrying, with her husband, after us, and in her arms she carried the babe she had just given birth to. Her husband and herself, between them, managed to carry that infant to the end of the retreat, where we embarked. God tempers the wind, it is said, to the shorn lamb; and many years afterwards I saw that boy, a strong and healthy lad. The woman's name was M'Guire, a sturdy and hardy Irishwoman; and lucky was it for herself and babe that she was so, as that night of cold and sleet was in itself sufficient to try the constitution of most females. I lost sight of her, I recollect, on this night, when the darkness came upon us; but with the dawn, to my surprise, she was still amongst us.

The shoes and boots of our party were now mostly either destroyed or useless to us, from foul roads and long miles, and many of the men were entirely barefooted, with knapsacks and accoutrements altogether in a dilapidated state. The officers were also, for the most part, in as miserable a plight. They were pallid, way-worn, their feet bleeding, and their faces overgrown with beards of many days' growth. What a contrast did our corps display, even at this period of the retreat, to my remembrance of them on the morning their dashing appearance captivated my fancy in Ireland! Many of the poor fellows, now near sinking with fatigue, reeled as if in a state of drunkenness, and altogether I thought we looked the ghosts of our former selves; still we held on resolutely: our officers behaved nobly; and Craufurd was not to be daunted by long miles, fatigue, or fine weather. Many a man in that retreat caught courage from his stern eye and gallant bearing. Indeed, I do not think the world ever saw a more perfect soldier than General Craufurd. It might be on the night following the disaster I have just narrated that we came to a halt for about a couple of hours in a small village, and together with several others, I sought shelter in the stable of a sort of farm-house, the first roof I saw near. Here, however, we found nothing to refresh ourselves with, by way of food, but some raw potatoes lying in a heap in one of the empty stalls, and which, for want of better rations, we made a meal of, before we threw ourselves down upon the stones with which the place was paved. Meanwhile, others of the men, together with two or three of our officers, more fortunate than ourselves, had possession of the rooms of the adjoining building, where they found at least a fire to warm themselves.

Lieutenant Hill had a black servant with him in this retreat, a youth he had brought with him from Monte Video, where, I heard, the Rifles had found him tied to a gun they had captured there. This lad came and aroused me as I lay in the mule-stable, and desired me to speak with his master in the adjoining room. I found the lieutenant seated in a chair by the fire when I entered. He was one of the few amongst us who rejoiced in the possession of a tolerably decent pair of boots, and he had sent for me to put a few stitches in them, in order to keep them from flying to pieces. I was so utterly wearied that I at first refused to have anything to do with them; but the officer, taking off his boots, insisted upon my getting out my wax threads and mending them; and himself and servant, thrusting me into the chair he arose from, put the boots into my hands, got out my shoemaking implements, and held me up as I attempted to cobble up the boots. It was, however, in vain that I tried to do my best towards the lieutenant's boots. After a few stitches, I fell asleep as I worked, the awl and wax-ends falling to the ground. I remember there were two other officers present at the time, Lieutenants Molloy and Keppel, the latter of whom soon afterwards fell dead from fatigue during this retreat. At the present time, however, they all saw it was in vain to urge me to mend Lieutenant Hill's boots. He therefore put them on again with a woeful face and a curse, and dismissed me to my repose. Our rest was not, however, of long duration. The French were upon our trail, and before long we were up and hurrying onwards again.

As the day began to dawn, we passed through another village—a long, straggling place. The houses were all closed at this early hour, and the inhabitants mostly buried in sleep, and, I dare say, unconscious of the armed thousands who were pouring through their silent streets. When about a couple of miles from this village, Craufurd again halted us for about a quarter of an hour. It appeared to me that, with returning daylight, he wished to have a good look at us this morning, for he mingled amongst the men as we stood leaning upon our rifles, gazing earnestly in our faces as he passed, in order to judge of our plight by our countenances. He himself appeared anxious, but full of fire and spirit, occasionally giving directions to the different officers, and then speaking words of encouragement to the men. It is my pride now to remember that General Craufurd seldom omitted a word in passing to myself. On this occasion he stopped in the midst and addressed a few words to me, and glancing down at my feet, observed:

'What! no shoes, Harris, I see, eh?'

'None, sir,' I replied; 'they have been gone many days back.' He smiled, and passing on, spoke to another man, and so on through the whole body.

Craufurd was, I remember, terribly severe, during this retreat, if he caught anything like pilfering amongst the men. As we stood, however, during this short halt, a very tempting turnip-field was close on the side of us, and several of the men were so ravenous, that although he was in our very ranks, they stepped into the field and helped themselves to the turnips, devouring them like famishing wolves. He either did not or would not observe the delinquency this time, and soon afterwards gave the word, and we moved on once more.

About this period I remember another sight, which I shall not to my dying day forget; and it causes me a sore heart, even now, as I remember it. Soon after our halt beside the turnip-field the screams of a child near me caught my ear, and drew my attention to one of our women, who was endeavouring to drag along a little boy of about seven or eight years of age. The poor child was apparently completely exhausted, and his legs failing under him. The mother had occasionally, up to this time, been assisted by some of the men, taking it in turn to help the little fellow on; but now all further appeal was vain. No man had more strength than was necessary for the support of his own carcass, and the mother could no longer raise the child in her arms, as her reeling pace too plainly showed. Still, however, she continued to drag the child along with her. It was a pitiable sight, and wonderful to behold the efforts the poor woman made to keep the boy amongst us. At last the little fellow had not even strength to cry, but, with mouth wide open, stumbled onwards, until both sank down to rise no more. The poor woman herself had, for some time, looked a moving corpse; and when the shades of evening came down, they were far behind amongst the dead or dying in the road. This was not the only scene of the sort I witnessed amongst the women and children during that retreat. Poor creatures! they must have bitterly regretted not having accepted the offer which was made to them to embark at Lisbon for England, instead of accompanying their husbands into Spain. The women, however, I have often observed, are most persevering in such cases, and are not to be persuaded that their presence is often a source of anxiety to the corps they belong to.

I do not think I ever admired any man who wore the British uniform more than I did General Craufurd.

I could fill a book with descriptions of him; for I frequently had my eye upon him in the hurry of action. It was gratifying to me, too, to think he did not altogether think ill of me, since he has often addressed me kindly when, from adverse circumstances, you might have thought that he had scarcely spirits to cheer up the men under him. The Rifles liked him, but they also feared him; for he could be terrible when insubordination showed itself in the ranks. 'You think, because you are Riflemen, you may do whatever you think proper,' said he one day to the miserable and savage-looking crew around him in the retreat to Coruña; 'but I'll teach you the difference before I have done with you.' I remember one evening, during the retreat, he detected two men straying away from the main body: it was in the early stage of that disastrous flight, and Craufurd knew well that he must do his utmost to keep the division together. He halted the brigade with a voice of thunder, ordered a drum-head court-martial on the instant, and they were sentenced to a hundred a-piece. Whilst this hasty trial was taking place, Craufurd, dismounting from his horse, stood in the midst, looking stern and angry as a worried bulldog. He did not like retreating at all, that man.

The three men nearest him, as he stood, were Jagger, Dan Howans, and myself. All were worn, dejected, and savage, though nothing to what we were after a few days more of the retreat. The whole brigade were in a grumbling and discontented mood; and Craufurd, doubtless, felt ill-pleased with the aspect of affairs altogether.

'D—n his eyes!' muttered Howans, 'he had much better try to get us something to eat and drink than harass us in this way.'

No sooner had Howans disburdened his conscience of this growl, than Craufurd, who had overheard it, turning sharply round, seized the rifle out of Jagger's hand, and felled him to the earth with the butt-end.

'It was not I who spoke,' said Jagger, getting up, and shaking his head. 'You shouldn't knock me about.'

'I heard you, sir,' said Craufurd; 'and I will bring you also to a court-martial.'

'I am the man who spoke,' said Howans. 'Ben Jagger never said a word.'

'Very well,' returned Craufurd, 'then I'll try you, sir.'

And, accordingly, when the other affair was disposed of, Howans' case came on. By the time the three men were tried, it was too dark to inflict the punishment. Howans, however, had got the complement of three hundred promised to him; so Craufurd gave the word to the brigade to move on. He marched all that night on foot; and when the morning dawned, I remember that, like the rest of us, his hair, beard, and eyebrows were covered with the frost as if he had grown white with age. We were, indeed, all of us in the same condition. Scarcely had I time to notice the appearance of morning before the general once more called a halt – we were then on the hills. Ordering a square to be formed, he spoke to the brigade, as well as I can remember, in these words, after having ordered the three before-named men of the 95th to be brought into the square:

'Although,' said he, 'I should obtain the goodwill neither of the officers nor the men of the brigade here by so doing, I am resolved to punish these three men, according to the sentence awarded, even though the French are at our heels. Begin with Daniel Howans.'

This was indeed no time to be lax in discipline, and the general knew it. The men, as I said, were, some of them, becoming careless and ruffianly in their demeanour; whilst others again I saw with the tears falling down their cheeks from the agony of their bleeding feet, and many were ill with dysentery from the effects of the bad food they had got hold of and devoured on the road. Our knapsacks, too, were a bitter enemy on this prolonged march. Many a man died, I am convinced, who would have borne up well to the end of the retreat but for the infernal load we carried on our backs. My own knapsack was my bitterest enemy; I felt it press me to the earth almost at times, and more than once felt as if I should die under its deadly embrace. The knapsacks, in my opinion, should have been abandoned at the very commencement of the retrograde movement, as it would have been better to have lost them altogether, if, by such loss, we could have saved the poor fellows who, as it was, died strapped to them on the road.

There was some difficulty in finding a place to tie Howans up, as the light brigade carried no halberts. However, they led him to a slender ash tree which grew near at hand.

'Don't trouble yourselves about tying *me* up,' said Howans, folding him arms; 'I'll take my punishment like a man!'

He did so without a murmur, receiving the whole three hundred. His wife, who was present with us, I remember, was a strong, hardy Irishwoman. When it was over, she stepped up and covered Howans with his grey great-coat. The general then gave the word to move on. I rather think he knew the enemy was too near to punish the other two delinquents just then; so we proceeded out of the cornfield in which we had been halted, and toiled away upon the hills once more, Howans' wife carrying the jacket, knapsack, and pouch, which the lacerated state of the man's back would not permit him to bear.

It could not have been, I should think, more than an hour after the punishment had been inflicted upon Howans, when the general again gave the word for the brigade to halt, and once more formed them into square. We had begun to suppose that he intended to allow the other two delinquents to escape under the present difficulties and hardships of the retreat. He was not, however, one of the forgetful sort, when the discipline of the army under him made severity necessary.

'Bring out the two other men of the 95th,' said he, 'who were tried last night.'

The men were brought forth accordingly, and their lieutenant-colonel, Hamilton Wade, at the same time stepped forth. He walked up to the general, and lowering his sword, requested that he would forgive these men, as they were both of them good soldiers, and had fought in all the battles of Portugal.

'I order *you*, sir,' said the general, 'to do your duty. These men shall be punished.'

The lieutenant-colonel, therefore, recovering his sword, turned about, and fell back to the front of the Rifles. One of the men, upon this (I think it was Armstrong), immediately began to unstrap his knapsack and prepare for the lash. Craufurd had turned about meanwhile, and walked up to one side of the square. Apparently he suddenly relented a little, and, again turning sharp round, returned towards the two prisoners. 'Stop,' said he. 'In consequence of the intercession of your lieutenant-colonel, I will allow you thus much: you shall draw lots, and the winner shall escape; but one of the two I am determined to make an example of.'

The square was formed in a stubble-field, and the sergeant-major of the Rifles, immediately stooping down, plucked up two straws, and the men, coming forward, drew. I cannot be quite certain, but I think it was Armstrong who drew the longest straw, and won the safety of his hide; and his fellow gamester was in quick time tied to a tree, and the punishment commenced. A hundred was the sentence; but when the bugler had counted seventy-five, the general granted him a further indulgence, and ordered him to be taken down, and to join his company. The general calling for his horse now mounted for the first time for many hours, for he had not ridden all night, not, indeed, since the drum-head court-martial had taken place. Before he put the brigade in motion again, he gave us another short specimen of his eloquence, pretty much, I remember, after this style:

'I give you all notice,' said he, 'that I will halt the brigade again the very first moment I perceive any man disobeying my orders, and try him by court-martial on the spot.' He then gave us the word, and we resumed our march.

Many who read this, especially in these peaceful times, may suppose this was a cruel and unnecessary severity under the dreadful and harassing circumstances of that retreat; but I, who was there, and was, besides, a common soldier of the very regiment to which these men belonged, say *it was quite necessary*. No man but one formed of stuff like General Craufurd could have saved the brigade from perishing altogether; and, if he flogged two, he saved hundreds from death by his management. I detest the sight of the lash; but I am convinced the British army can never go on without it. Late events have taught us the necessity of such measures.

It was perhaps a couple of days after this had taken place that we came to a river. It was tolerably wide, but not very deep, which was just as well for us; for, had it been deep as the dark regions, we must have somehow or other got through. The avenger was behind us, and Craufurd was along with us, and the two together kept us moving, whatever was in the road. Accordingly into the stream went the light brigade, and Craufurd, as busy as a shepherd with his flock, riding in and out of the water to keep his wearied band from being drowned as they crossed over. Presently he spied an officer who, to save himself from being wet through, I suppose, and wearing a damp pair of breeches for the remainder of the day, had mounted on the back of one of his men. The sight of such a piece of effeminacy was enough to raise the choler of the general, and in a very short time he was plunging and splashing through the water after them both.

'Put him down, sir! put him down! I desire you to put that officer down instantly!' And the soldier in an instant, I dare say nothing loth, dropping his burden like a hot potato into the stream, continued his progress through. 'Return back, sir,' said Craufurd to the officer, 'and go through the water like the others. I will not allow my officers to ride upon the men's backs through the rivers: all must take their share alike here.'

Wearied as we were, this affair caused all who saw it to shout almost with laughter, and was never forgotten by those who survived the retreat.

General Craufurd was, indeed, one of the few men who was apparently created for command during such dreadful scenes as we were familiar with in this retreat. He seemed an iron man; nothing daunted him – nothing turned him from his purpose. War was his very element, and toil and danger seemed to call forth only an increasing determination to surmount them. I was sometimes amused with his appearance, and that of the men around us; for, the Rifles being always at his heels, he seemed to think them his familiars. If he stopped his horse, and halted to deliver one of his stern reprimands, you would see half a dozen lean, unshaven, shoeless, and savage Riflemen standing for the moment leaning upon their weapons, and scowling up in his face as he scolded; and when he dashed the spurs into his reeking horse, they would throw up their rifles upon their shoulders, and hobble after him again. He was sometimes to be seen in the front, then in the rear, and then you would fall in with him again in the midst, dismounted, and marching on foot, that the men might see he took an equal share in the toils which they were enduring. He had a mortal dislike, I remember, to a commissary. Many a time have I heard him storming at the neglect of those gentry when the men were starving for rations, and nothing but excuses forthcoming.

'Send the commissary to me!' he would roar. 'D—n him! I will hang him if the provisions are not up this night!'

Twice I remember he was in command of the light brigade. The second time he joined them he made, I heard, something like these remarks, after they had been some little time in Spain:

'When I commanded you before,' he said, 'I know full well that you disliked me, for you thought me severe. *This time I am glad to find there is a change in yourselves.*'

13

TOWARDS evening of the same day Howans was punished, we came to a part of the country of a yet wilder and more desolate appearance even than that we had already traversed; a dreary wilderness it appeared at this inclement season: and our men, spite of the vigilance of the general, seemed many of them resolved to stray into the open country rather than traverse the road before them. The coming night favoured their designs, and many were, before morning, lost to us through their own wilfulness. Amongst others, I found myself completely bewildered and lost upon the heath, and should doubtless have perished had I not fallen in with another of our corps in the same situation. As soon as we recognised each other, I found my companion in adversity was a strapping resolute fellow named James Brooks, a north of Ireland man. He was afterwards killed at Toulouse by a musket-ball which struck him in the thigh. He was delighted at having met with me, and we resolved not to desert each other during the night. Brooks, as I have said, was a strong, active, and resolute fellow as indeed I had, on more occasions than one, witnessed in Portugal. At the present time his strength was useful to both of us.

'Catch hold of my jacket, Harris,' said he: 'the ground here is soft, and we must help each other to-night, or we shall be lost in the bogs.'

Before long, that which Brooks feared, happened, and he found himself stuck so fast in the morass, that although I used my best efforts to draw him out I only shared in the same disaster; so that, leaving him, I turned and endeavoured to save my own life if possible, calling to him to follow before he sank over head and ears. This was an unlucky chance in our wearied state, as the more we floundered in the dark, not knowing which way to gain a firmer foundation, the faster we fixed ourselves. Poor Brooks was so disheartened, that he actually blubbered like a child. At length, during a pause in our exertions, I thought I heard something like the bark of a dog come down the wind. I bade Brooks listen, and we both distinctly heard it – the sound gave us new hope, just as we were about to abandon ourselves to our fate. I advised Brooks to lay himself as flat as he could, and drag himself out of the slough, as I had found some hard tufts of grass in the direction I tried; and so, by degrees, we gained a firmer footing, and eventually succeeded in extricating ourselves, though in such an exhausted state, that for some time we lay helplessly upon the ground, unable to proceed.

At length with great caution, we ventured to move forwards in the direction of the sounds we had just heard. We found, however, that our situation was still very perilous; for in the darkness we hardly dared to move a step in any direction without probing the ground with our rifles, lest we should again sink, and be eventually smothered in the morasses we had strayed amongst. On a sudden, however (as we carefully felt our way), we heard voices shouting in the distance, and calling out '*Men* lost! *men* lost!' which we immediately concluded were the cries of some of our own people, who were situated like ourselves.

After awhile I thought I saw, far away, something like a dancing light, which seemed to flicker about, vanish, and reappear, similar to a Jack-o'-lantern. I pointed it out to Brooks, and we agreed to alter our course, and move towards it. As we did so, the light seemed to approach us, and grow larger, and presently another and another appeared, like small twinkling stars, till they looked something like the lamps upon one of our London bridges, as seen from afar. The sight revived our spirits, more especially as we could now distinctly hear the shouts of people, who appeared in search of the stragglers, and as they approached us, we perceived that such was indeed the case. The lights, we now discovered, were furnished by bundles of straw and dried twigs, tied on the ends of long poles, and dipped in tar. They were borne in the hands of several Spanish peasants, from a village near at hand, whom Craufurd had thus sent to our rescue.

He had discovered, on reaching and halting in this village, the number of men that had strayed from the main body, and immediately ordering the torches I have mentioned to be prepared, he collected together a party of Spanish peasants, and obliged them to go out into the open country, and seek for his men, as I have said; by which means he saved (on that night) many from death.

To return to my own adventures on this night. When Brooks and myself reached the village I have mentioned we found it filled with soldiers, standing and lying, huddled together like cattle in a fair. A most extraordinary sight it appeared as the torches of the peasants flashed upon the way-worn and gaunt figures of our army. The rain was coming down, too, on this night, I remember; and soon after I reached our corps, I fell helplessly to the ground in a miserable plight. Brooks was himself greatly exhausted, but he behaved nobly, and remained beside me, trying to persuade some of our men to assist him in lifting me up, and gaining shelter in one of the houses at hand. 'May I be—!' I heard him say, 'if I leave Harris to be butchered in the streets by the cowardly Spaniards the moment our division leaves the town.' At length Brooks succeeded in getting a man to help him, and together they supported me into the passage of a house, where I lay upon the floor for some time. After awhile, by the help of some wine they procured, I rallied and sat up, till eventually I got once more upon my legs, and, arm in arm, we proceeded again into the streets, and joined our corps. Poor Brooks certainly saved my life that night. He was one of the many good fellows whom I have seen out, and I often think of him with feelings of gratitude as I sit at my work in Richmond Street, Soho.

When the division got the order to proceed again, we were still linked arm in arm, and thus we proceeded; sometimes, when the day appeared, stopping for a short time and resting ourselves, and then hurrying on again.

I remember Sir Dudley Hill passing me on a mule this day. He wore a Spanish straw-hat, and had his cloak on. He looked back when he had passed, and addressed me. 'Harris,' said he, 'I see you cannot keep up.' He appeared sorry for me, for he knew me well. 'You must do your best,' he said, 'my man, and keep with us, or you will fall into the hands of the enemy.' As the day wore on, I grew weaker and weaker; and at last, spite of all my efforts, I saw the main body leave me hopelessly in the lurch. Brooks himself was getting weaker too; he saw it was of little use to urge me on, and at length, assenting to my repeated request to be left behind, he hurried on as well as he was able without a word of farewell. I now soon sank down in the road and lay beside another man who had also fallen, and was apparently dead, and whom I recognised as one of our sergeants, named Taylor, belonging to the Honourable Captain Pakenham's (now General Sir Hercules Pakenham) company.

14

WHILST we lay exhausted in the road, the rear guard, which was now endeavouring to drive on the stragglers, approached, and a sergeant of the Rifles came up and stopped to look at us. He addressed himself to me, and ordered me to rise; but I told him it was useless for him to trouble himself about me, as I was unable to move a step further. Whilst he was urging me to endeavour to rise up, the officer in command of the rear guard also stepped up. The name of this officer was Lieutenant Cox; he was a brave and good man, and observing that the sergeant was rough in his language and manner towards me, he silenced him, and bade the guard proceed, and leave me. 'Let him die quietly, Hicks,' he said to the sergeant. 'I know him well; he's not the man to lie here if he could get on. I am sorry, Harris,' he said, 'to see you reduced to this, for I fear there is no help to be had now.' He then moved on after his men, and left me to my fate.

After lying still for awhile, I felt somewhat restored, and sat up to look about me. The sight was by no means cheering. On the road behind me I saw men, women, mules, and horses, lying at intervals, both dead and dying; whilst far away in front I could just discern the enfeebled army crawling out of sight, the women huddled together in its rear, trying their best to get forward amongst those of the sick soldiery, who were now unable to keep up with the main body. Some of these poor wretches cut a ludicrous figure, having the men's great-coats buttoned over their heads, whilst their clothing being extremely ragged and scanty, their naked legs were very conspicuous. They looked a tribe of travelling beggars. [Footnote in original edition.] After awhile, I found that my companion, the sergeant, who lay beside me, had also recovered a little, and I tried to cheer him up. I told him that opposite to where we were lying there was a lane down which we might possibly find some place of shelter, if we could muster strength to explore it. The sergeant consented to make the effort, but after two or three attempts to rise, gave it up. I myself was more fortunate: with the aid of my rifle I got upon my legs, and seeing death in my companion's face, I resolved to try and save myself, since it was quite evident to me that I could render him no assistance.

After hobbling some distance down the lane, to my great joy I espied a small hut or cabin, with a little garden in its front; I therefore opened the small door of the hovel, and was about to enter, when I considered that most likely I should be immediately knocked on the head by the inmates if I did so. The rain, I remember, was coming down in torrents at this time, and, reflecting that to remain outside was but to die, I resolved at all events to try my luck within. I had not much strength left; but I resolved to sell myself as dearly as I could. I therefore brought up my rifle, and stepped across the threshold. As soon as I had done so, I observed an old woman seated beside a small fire upon the hearth. She turned her head as I entered, and immediately upon seeing a strange soldier, she arose, and filled the hovel with her screams. As I drew back within the doorway, an elderly man, followed by two, who were apparently his sons, rushed from a room in the interior. They immediately approached me; but I brought up my rifle again, and cocked it, bidding them keep their distance.

After I had thus brought them to a parley, I got together what little Spanish I was master of, and begged for shelter for the night and a morsel of food, at the same time lifting my feet and displaying them a mass of bleeding sores. It was not, however, till they had held a tolerably long conversation among themselves that they consented to afford me shelter; and then only upon the condition that I left by daylight on the following morning. I accepted the conditions with joy. Had they refused me, I should indeed not have been here to tell the tale. Knowing the treachery of the Spanish character, I however refused to relinquish possession of my rifle, and my right hand was ready in an instant to unsheath my bayonet as they sat and stared at me whilst I devoured the food they offered.

All they gave me was some coarse black bread, and a pitcher of sour wine. It was, however, acceptable to a half-famished man; and I felt greatly revived by it. Whilst I supped, the old hag, who sat close beside the hearth, stirred up the embers that they might have a better view of their guest, and the party meanwhile overwhelmed me with questions, which I could neither comprehend nor had strength to answer. I soon made signs to them that I was unable to maintain the conversation, and begged of them, as well as I could, to show me some place where I might lay my wearied limbs till dawn.

Notwithstanding the weariness which pervaded my whole body, I was unable for some time to sleep except by fitful snatches, such was the fear I entertained of having my throat cut by the savage-looking wretches still seated before the fire. Besides which, the place they had permitted me to crawl into was more like an oven than anything else, and being merely a sort of berth scooped out of the wall was so filled with fleas and other vermin that I was stung and tormented most miserably all night long.

Bad as they had been, however, I felt somewhat restored by my lodging and supper, and with the dawn I crawled out of my lair, left the hut, retraced my steps along the lane, and once more emerged upon the high-road, where I found my companion, the sergeant, dead, and lying where I had left him the night before.

I now made the best of my way along the road in the direction in which I had last seen our army retreating the night before. A solitary individual, I seemed left behind amongst those who had perished. It was still raining, I remember, on this morning, and the very dead looked comfortless in their last sleep, as I passed them occasionally lying on the line of march.

It had pleased Heaven to give me an iron constitution, or I must have failed, I think, on this day, for the solitary journey and the miserable spectacles I beheld rather damped my spirits.

After progressing some miles, I came up with a cluster of poor devils who were still alive, but apparently, both men and women, unable to proceed. They were sitting huddled together in the road, their heads drooping forward, and apparently patiently awaiting their end.

Soon after passing these unfortunates, I overtook a party who were being urged forward under charge of an officer of the 42nd Highlanders. He was pushing them along pretty much as a drover would keep together a tired flock of sheep. They presented a curious example of a retreating force. Many of them had thrown away their weapons, and were linked together arm in arm, in order to support each other, like a party of drunkards. They were, I saw, composed of various regiments; many were bare-headed, and without shoes; and some with their heads tied up in old rags and fragments of handkerchiefs.

I marched in company with this party for some time, but as I felt after my night's lodging and refreshment in better condition I ventured to push forwards, in the hope of rejoining the main body, and which I once more came up with in the streets of a village.

On falling in with the Rifles I again found Brooks, who was surprised at seeing me still alive; and we both entered a house, and begged for something to drink. I remember that I had a shirt upon my back at this time, which I had purchased of a drummer of the 9th regiment before the commencement of the retreat. It was the only good one I had; I stripped, with the assistance of Brooks, and took it off, and exchanged it with a Spanish woman for a loaf of bread, which Brooks, myself, and two other men shared amongst us.

I remember to have again remarked Craufurd at this period of the retreat. He was no whit altered in his desire to keep the force together I thought; but still active and vigilant as ever he seemed to keep his eye upon those who were now most likely to hold out. I myself marched during many hours close beside him this day. He looked stern and pale; but the very picture of a warrior. I shall never forget Craufurd if I live to a hundred years I think. He was in everything a soldier.

Slowly and dejectedly crawled our army along. Their spirit of endurance was now considerably worn out, and judging from my own sensations, I felt confident that if the sea was much further from us, we must be content to come to a halt at last without gaining it. I felt something like the approach of death as I proceeded – a sort of horror, mixed up with my sense of illness – a reeling I have never experienced before or since. Still I held on; but with all my efforts, the main body again left me behind. Had the enemy's cavalry come up at this time I think they would have had little else to do but ride us down without striking a blow.

It is, however, indeed astonishing how man clings to life. I am certain that had I lain down at this period, I should have found my last billet on the spot I sank upon. Suddenly I heard a shout in front, which was prolonged in a sort of hubbub. Even the stragglers whom I saw dotting the road in front of me seemed to have caught at something like hope; and as the poor fellows now reached the top of a hill we were ascending, I heard an occasional exclamation of joy – the first note of the sort I had heard for many days. When I reached the top of the hill the thing spoke for itself. There, far away in our front, the English shipping lay in sight.

Its view had indeed acted like a restorative to our force, and the men, at the prospect of a termination to the march, had plucked up spirit for a last effort. Fellows who, like myself, seemed to have hardly strength in their legs to creep up the ascent seemed now to have picked up a fresh pair to get down with. Such is hope to us poor mortals!

There was, I recollect, a man of the name of Bell, of the Rifles, who had been during this day holding a sort of creeping race with me – we had passed and repassed each other, as our strength served. Bell was rather a discontented fellow at the best of times; but during this retreat he had given full scope to his ill-temper, cursing the hour he was born, and wishing his mother had strangled him when he came into the world, in order to have saved him from his present toil. He had not now spoken for some time, and the sight of the English shipping had apparently a very beneficial effect upon him. He burst into tears as he stood and looked at it.

'Harris,' he said, 'if it pleases God to let me reach those ships, I swear never to utter a bad or discontented word again.'

As we proceeded down the hill we now met with the first symptoms of good feeling from the inhabitants it was our fortune to experience during our retreat. A number of old women stood on either side of the road, and occasionally handed us fragments of bread as we passed them. It was on this day, and whilst I looked anxiously upon the English shipping in the distance, that I first began to find my eye-sight failing, and it appeared to me that I was fast growing blind. The thought was alarming; and I made desperate efforts to get on. Bell, however, won the race this time. He was a very athletic and strong-built fellow, and left me far behind, so that I believe at that time I was the very last of the retreating force that reached the beach, though doubtless many stragglers came dropping up after the ships had sailed, and were left behind.

As it was, when I did manage to gain the sea-shore, it was only by the aid of my rifle that I could stand, and my eyes were now so dim and heavy that with difficulty I made out a boat which seemed the last that had put off.

Fearful of being left half blind in the lurch, I took off my cap, and placed it on the muzzle of my rifle as a signal, for I was totally unable to call out. Luckily, Lieutenant Cox, who was aboard the boat, saw me, and ordered the men to return, and, making one more effort, I walked into the water, and a sailor stretching his body over the gunwale, seized me as if I had been an infant, and hauled me on board. His words were characteristic of the English sailor, I thought.

'Hollo there, you lazy lubber!' he said, as he grasped hold

of me, 'who the h—ll do you think is to stay humbugging all day for such a fellow as you?'

The boat, I found, was crowded with our exhausted men, who lay helplessly at the bottom, the heavy sea every moment drenching them to the skin. As soon as we reached the vessel's side, the sailors immediately aided us to get on board, which in our exhausted state was not a very easy matter, as they were obliged to place ropes in our hands, and heave us up by setting their shoulders under us, and hoisting away as if they had been pushing bales of goods on board.

'Heave away!' cried one of the boat's crew, as I clung to a rope, quite unable to pull myself up, 'heave away, you lubber!'

The tar placed his shoulder beneath me as he spoke, and hoisted me up against the ship's side; I lost my grasp of the rope and should have fallen into the sea had it not been for two of the crew. These men grasped me as I was falling, and drew me into the port-hole like a bundle of foul clothes, tearing away my belt and bayonet in the effort, which fell into the sea.

It was not very many minutes after I was on board, for I lay where the sailors had first placed me after dragging me through the port-hole, ere I was sound asleep. I slept long and heavily, and it was only the terrible noise and bustle on board consequent upon a gale having sprung up, that at length awoke me. The wind increased as the night came on, and soon we had to experience all the horrors of a storm at sea. The pumps were set to work; the sails were torn to shreds; the coppers were overset; and we appeared in a fair way, I thought, of going to the bottom. Meanwhile, the pumps were kept at work night and day incessantly till they were choked; and the gale growing worse and worse, all the soldiery were ordered below, and the hatches closed; soon after which the vessel turned over on one side, and lay a helpless log upon the water. In this situation an officer was placed over us, with his sword drawn in one hand, and a lantern in the other, in order to keep us on the side which was uppermost, so as to give the vessel a chance of righting herself in the roaring tide. The officer's task was not an easy one as the heaving waves frequently sent us sprawling from the part we clung to, over to the lowermost part of the hold where he stood, and he was obliged every minute to drive us back.

We remained in this painful situation for, I should think, five or six hours, expecting every instant to be our last, when, to our great joy, the sea suddenly grew calm, the wind abated, the vessel righted herself, and we were once more released from our prison, having tasted nothing in the shape of food for at least forty-eight hours. Soon after this we arrived in sight of Spithead, where we saw nine of our convoy, laden with troops, which had been driven on shore in the gale. After remaining off Spithead for about five or six days, one fine morning we received orders to disembark, and our poor bare feet once more touched English ground. The inhabitants flocked down to the beach to see us as we did so, and they must have been a good deal surprised at the spectacle we presented. Our beards were long and ragged; almost all were without shoes and stockings; many had their clothes and accoutrements in fragments, with their heads swathed in old rags, and our weapons were covered with rust; whilst not a few had now, from toil and fatigue, become quite blind.

Let not the reader, however, think that even now we were to be despised as soldiers. Long marches, inclement weather, and want of food, had done their work upon us; but we were perhaps better than we appeared, as the sequel showed. Under the gallant Craufurd we had made some tremendous marches, and even galled our enemies severely making good our retreat by the way of Vigo. But our comrades in adversity, and who had retired by the other road to Coruña, under General Moore, turned to bay there, and showed the enemy that the English soldier is not to be beaten even under the most adverse circumstances.

The field of death and slaughter, the march, the bivouac, and the retreat, are no bad places in which to judge of men. I have had some opportunities of judging them in all these situations, and I should say that the British are amongst the most splendid soldiers in the world. Give them fair play, and they are unconquerable. For my own part I can only say that I enjoyed life more whilst on active service than I have ever done since; and as I sit at work in my shop in Richmond Street, Soho, I look back upon that portion of my time spent in the fields of the Peninsula as the only part worthy of remembrance. It is at such times that scenes long passed come back upon my mind as if they had taken place but yesterday. I remember even the very appearance of some of the regiments engaged; and comrades, long mouldered to dust, I see again performing the acts of heroes.

15

AFTER the disastrous retreat to Coruña, the Rifles were reduced to a sickly skeleton, if I may so term it. Out of perhaps nine hundred of as active and fine fellows as ever held a weapon in the field of an enemy's country, we paraded some three hundred weak and crestfallen invalids.

I myself stood the third man in my own company, which was reduced from near a hundred men to *but three*. Indeed, I think we had scarce a company on parade stronger than ten or twelve men at the first parade. After a few parades, however, our companies gradually were augmented (by those of the sick who recovered), but many of those who did not sink in hospital were never more of much service as soldiers.

The captain of my company was sick, and Lieutenant Hill commanded the three men who answered for No. 4 on this occasion.

I remember he smiled when he looked at me. 'Harris,' he said, 'you look the best man here this morning. You seem to have got over this business well.'

'Yes, sir,' I said, 'thank God I feel pretty stout again now, which is more than many can say.'

Both battalions of the Rifles had been in that retreat. The first battalion lay at Colchester at this time. Ours (the second) was quartered at Hythe. Colonel Beckwith* commanded the

* Thomas Sydney Beckwith (1772–1831). One of the finest commanders of light troops in the history of the Army, he was with the 1st Battalion of the 95th throughout the campaign. He

first and Colonel Wade the second. I remember the 43rd and 52nd regiments paraded with our battalion on this occasion at Hythe, and both having been with us on the Coruña retreat cut as poor a figure as we ourselves did.

After awhile, some of the strongest and smartest of our men were picked out to go on the recruiting service, and gather men from the militia regiments to fill up our ranks. I myself started off with Lieutenant Pratt, Sergeant-major Adams, and William Brotherwood, the latter of whom was afterwards killed at Vittoria by a cannon-ball, which at the same moment ended Patrick Mahon and Lieutenant Hopwood.*

I was a shoemaker in the corps, and had twenty pounds in my pocket which I had saved up. With this money I hired a gig, and the sergeant-major and myself cut a very smart figure. The only difficulty was that neither of us knew how to drive very well, consequently we overturned the gig on the first day, before we got half-way on our journey, and the shafts being broken we were obliged to leave it behind us in a small village midway between Hythe and Rye, and take to our legs, as was more soldierlike and seemly. We reached Rye the same night, and I recollect that I succeeded in getting the first recruit there, a strong, able-bodied chimney-sweep named John Lee. This fellow (whose appearance I was struck with as he sat in the tap-room of the 'Red Lion' on that night, together with a little boy as black and sooty as himself) offered to enlist the moment I entered the room, and I took him at his word, and immediately called for the sergeant-major for approval.

'There's nothing against my being a soldier,' said the sweep, 'but my black face; I'm strong, active, and healthy, and able to lick the best man in this room.'

'Hang your black face,' said the sergeant-major; 'the Rifles

was appointed commander-in-chief at Bombay in 1829, and promoted lieutenant-general in 1830.

* Brotherwood, Mahon and Hopwood were all killed by the same cannon-ball as they crept from cover in an attempt to shoot one of the French generals. It was not unknown for a ball to kill as many as ten men standing in file.

can't be too dark; you're a strong rascal, and if you mean it, we'll take you to the doctor to-morrow and make a giniril of you the next day.' So we had the sweep that night into a large tub of water, scoured him outside, and filled him with punch inside, and made a Rifleman of him.

The sergeant-major, however, on this night, suspected from his countenance, what afterwards turned out to be the case, that Lee was rather a slippery fellow, and might repent. So, after filling him drunk, he said to me – 'Harris, *you* have caught this bird, and *you* must keep him fast. You must both sleep to-night handcuffed together in the same bed, or he will escape us'; which I actually did, and the next morning re-traced my steps with him to Hythe, to be passed by the doctor of our regiment.

After rejoining Sergeant-major Adams at Rye, we started off for Hastings in Sussex, and on our way we heard of the East Kent Militia at Lydd; so we stopped there about an hour to display ourselves before them, and try if we could coax a few of them into the Rifles. We strutted up and down before their ranks arm in arm, and made no small sensation amongst them. When on the recruiting service in those days, men were accustomed to make as gallant a show as they could, and accordingly we had both smartened ourselves up a trifle. The sergeant-major was quite a beau in his way; he had a sling belt to his sword like a field-officer, a tremendous green feather in his cap, a flaring sash, his whistle and powder-flask displayed, an officer's pelisse over one shoulder, and a double allowance of ribbons in his cap; whilst I myself was also as smart as I dared appear, with my rifle slung at my shoulder.

In this guise we made as much of ourselves as if we had both been generals, and, as I said, created quite a sensation, the militia-men cheering us as we passed up and down, till they were called to order by the officers.

The permission to volunteer was not then given to the East Kent, although it came out a few days afterwards, and we persuaded many men, during the hour we figured before them, that the Rifles were the only boys fit for *them* to join.

After looking up the East Kent, we reached Hastings that

same night, where we found that the volunteering of the Leicester Militia (who were quartered there) had commenced, and that one hundred and twenty-five men and two officers had given their names to the 7th Fusileers, and these Adams and I determined to make change their minds in our favour if we could.

The appearance of our Rifle uniform, and a little of Sergeant Adams's blarney, so took the fancies of the volunteers, that we got everyone of them for the Rifle corps, and both officers into the bargain. We worked hard in this business. I may say that for three days and nights we kept up the dance and the drunken riot. Every volunteer got ten guineas bounty, which, except the two kept back for necessaries, they spent in every sort of excess, till all was gone. Then came the reaction. The drooping spirits, the grief at parting with old comrades, sweethearts, and wives, for the uncertain fate of war. And then came on the jeers of the old soldier; the laughter of Adams and myself, and comrades, and our attempts to give a fillip to their spirits as we marched them off from the friends they were never to look upon again; and as we termed it, 'shove them on to glory' – a glory they were not long in achieving, as out of the hundred and fifty of the Leicestershire which we enlisted in Hastings, scarce one man, I should say, who served, but could have shown at the year's end some token of the fields he had fought in; very many found a grave, and some returned to Hythe with the loss of their limbs.

I remember the story of many of these men's lives; that of one in particular named Demon, whom I myself enlisted from the Leicester Militia, is not a little curious. Demon was a smart and very active man, and serving as corporal in the light company of the Leicestershire when I persuaded him to join our corps, where he was immediately made a sergeant in the third battalion, then just forming; and from which he eventually rose to be a commissioned officer in one of our line regiments, but whose number I cannot now remember. The cause which led to Demon's merits being first noticed was not a little curious, being neither more nor less than a race.

It happened that at Shoreham Cliff (soon after he joined) a race was got up amongst some Kentish men, who were noted for their swiftness, and one of them, who had beaten his companions, challenged any soldier in the Rifles to run against him for two hundred pounds. The sum was large, and the runner was of so much celebrity, that although we had some active young fellows amongst us, no one seemed inclined to take the chance, either officers or men, till at length Demon stepped forth and said he would run against this Kentish boaster, or any man on the face of the earth, and fight him afterwards into the bargain, if anyone could be found to make up the money. Upon this, an officer subscribed the money, and the race was arranged.

The affair made quite a sensation, and the inhabitants of the different villages for miles around flocked to see the sport; besides which the men from different regiments in the neighbourhood, infantry, cavalry, and artillery, also were much interested, and managed to be present, which caused the scene to be a very gay one. In short, the race commenced, and the odds were much against the soldier at starting, as he was a much less man than the other, and did not at all look like the winner. He, however, kept well up with his antagonist, and the affair seemed likely to end in a dead heat, which would undoubtedly have been the case, but Demon, when close upon the winning-post, gave one tremendous spring forward, and won it by his body's length.

This race, in short, led on to notice and promotion. General Mackenzie* was in command of the garrison at Hythe. He

---

* Sir Kenneth Mackenzie (1754–1833). He had commanded the 52nd at Shorncliffe where a fall from his horse resulted in so severe a concussion that he was unable to accompany the regiment to the Peninsula. He was promoted major-general in 1811, however, and given command of all the light troops in England with his headquarters at Hythe. He took the name of Douglas – his mother's name – by royal licence in 1831.

was present, and was highly delighted at the Rifleman beating the bumpkin, and saw that the winner was the very cut of a soldier, and in short that Demon was a very smart fellow, so that, eventually, the news of the race reached the first battalion then fighting in Spain. Sir Andrew Barnard,* as far as I recollect from hearsay, at the time, was then in command of the Rifles in Spain; and, as I now remember the story, either he or some other officer of rank, upon being told of the circumstance, remarked that, as Demon was such a smart runner in England, there was very good ground for a Rifleman to use his legs in Spain. He was accordingly ordered out with the next draft to that country, where he so much distinguished himself that he obtained his commission, as already mentioned.

I could give many more anecdotes connected with the recruiting at this time for the three battalions of Rifles, but the above will suffice; and soon after the incident I have just narrated (our companies being full of young and active men), we started off with the expedition, then just formed, for Walcheren. I could not help feeling, when we paraded, that I stood enranked for this first expedition comparatively amongst strangers, since in the company I belonged to, not a single man, except James Brooks, whom I have before named, then paraded with me who had been a fellow comrade in the fields of Portugal and Spain. I felt also the loss of my old captain (Leech), whom I much loved and respected, and who left the second battalion at that time to be promoted in the first. When I heard of this change, I stepped from the ranks and offered to exchange into the first, but Lieutenant Hill, who was present, hinted to Captain Hart (my new commanding officer) not to let me go, as, if he did, he would perhaps repent it. I will not say here what the lieutenant then said of me, but he persuaded Captain Hart to keep me, as my charac-

* Sir Andrew Francis Barnard (1773–1855) exchanged into the 95th from the 1st Royals. He was appointed to the command of the 3rd Battalion of the 95th in 1810, and commanded the 2nd Brigade of the Light Division in 1814. He was knighted in 1815, and obtained the rank of general in 1851.

ter had been so good in the former campaign; and accordingly I remained in the second battalion, and started on the Walcheren expedition.*

From Hythe to Deal was one day's march; and I remember looking along the road at the good appearance the different regiments made as we marched along. It was as fine an expedition as ever I looked at, and the army seemed to stretch, as I regarded them, the whole distance before us to Dover.

* The disastrous expedition to the island of Walcheren at the mouth of the Scheldt was undertaken to help the Austrians by diverting Napoleon's attention from the Danube.

16

AT Deal, the Rifles embarked in the *Superb*, a seventy-four, and a terrible outcry there was amongst the women upon the beach on the embarkation; for the ill consequences of having too many women amongst us had been so apparent in our former campaign and retreat that the allowance of wives was considerably curtailed on this occasion, and the distraction of the poor creatures at parting with their husbands was quite heart-rending; some of them clinging to the men so resolutely, that the officers were obliged to give orders to have them separated by force. In fact, even after we were in the boats and fairly pushed off, the screaming and howling of their farewells rang in our ears far out at sea.

The weather being fair, and the fleet having a grand and imposing appearance, many spectators (even from London) came to look at us as we lay in the Downs, and we set sail (I think on the third day from our embarkation) in three divisions.

A fair wind soon carried us off Flushing where one part of the expedition disembarked; the other made for South Beveland, among which latter I myself was. The five companies of Rifles immediately occupied a very pretty village, with rows of trees on either side of its principal streets, where we had plenty of leisure to listen to the cannonading going on amongst the companies we had left at Flushing.

The appearance of the country (such as it was) was extremely pleasant, and for a few days the men enjoyed themselves much. But at the expiration of (I think) less time than a week, an awful visitation came suddenly upon us. The first I observed of it was one day as I sat in my billet, when I beheld whole parties of our Riflemen in the street shaking with a sort of ague, to such a degree that they could hardly walk; strong and fine young men who had been but a short time in the service seemed suddenly reduced in strength to infants, unable to stand upright—so great a shaking had seized upon their whole bodies from head to heel. The company I belonged to was quartered in a barn, and I quickly perceived that hardly a man there had stomach for the bread that was served out to him, or even to taste his grog, although each man had an allowance of half a pint of gin per day. In fact, I should say that, about three weeks from the day we landed, I and two others were the only individuals who could stand upon our legs. They lay groaning in rows in the barn, amongst the heaps of lumpy black bread they were unable to eat.

This awful spectacle considerably alarmed the officers, who were also many of them attacked. The naval doctors came on shore to assist the regimental surgeons, who, indeed, had more upon their hands than they could manage; Dr Ridgeway of the Rifles, and his assistant, having nearly five hundred patients prostrate at the same moment. In short, except myself and three or four others, the whole concern was completely floored.

Under these circumstances, which considerably confounded the doctors, orders were issued (since all hopes of getting the men upon their legs seemed gone) to embark them as fast as possible, which was accordingly done with some little difficulty. The poor fellows made every effort to get on board; those who were a trifle better than others crawled to the boats; many supported each other; and many were carried helpless as infants.

At Flushing matters were not much better, except that there the soldiers had a smart skirmish with their enemies before the fever and ague attacked them. On shipboard the aspect of affairs did not mend; the men beginning to die so fast that they committed ten or twelve to the deep in one day.

It was rather extraordinary that myself, and Brooks, and a man named Bowley, who had all three been at Coruña, were at this moment unattacked by the disease, and, notwithstanding the awful appearance of the pest-ship we were in, I myself had little fear of it, I thought myself so hardened that it could not touch me. It happened, however, that I stood sentinel (men being scarce) over the hatchway, and Brooks, who was always a jolly and jeering companion (even in the very jaws of death) came past me, and offered me a lump of pudding, it being pudding-day on board. At that moment I felt struck with a deadly faintness, shaking all over like an aspen, and my teeth chattering in my head so that I could hardly hold my rifle.

Brooks looked at me for a moment, with the pudding in his hand, which he saw I could not take. 'Hallo,' he said, 'why, Harris, old boy, *you* are not going to begin, are you?'

I felt unable to answer him, but only muttered out as I trembled, 'For God's sake get me relieved, Brooks!'

'Hallo?' said Brooks, 'it's all up with Harris! You're catched hold of at last, old chap.'

In fact I was soon sprawling upon the forecastle, amongst many others, in a miserable state, our knapsacks and our great-coats over us. In this state the doctors, during our short voyage, were fully employed; pails of infusion of bark were carried amongst us and given to the men in horn tumblers, and thus we arrived at Dover.

As I lay on the deck, I looked up at that splendid castle in the distance. It was identified with old England, and many a languid eye was cheered by its sight. Men naturally love to die upon their native land, and I felt I could now do so contentedly! Nay, I have that frowning English fortress in my eye at this moment as I then beheld it. The Warwickshire Militia were at this time quartered at Dover. They came to assist in disembarking us, and were obliged to lift many of us out of the boats like sacks of flour. If any of those militiamen remain alive, they will not easily forget that piece of duty; for I never beheld men more moved than they were at our helpless state. Many died at Dover and numbers in Deal; whilst those who had somewhat rallied on getting from the land of pestilence were paraded, in order to get them on to their old quarters at Hythe.

I remember that the 43rd and 52nd regiments (all that were able) marched with us this day to Hythe; but I'm afraid we did not (any of us) cut much of a figure on the road. In fact, such was the shaking fever we felt, we were left pretty much to our own discretion to get to our journey's end in the best manner we could. Many, indeed, would never have got into barracks without assistance. In short, when I sat down exhausted by the road-side several times during the march, and looked at the men, I thought it bore in some degree a similitude to the Coruña retreat, so awfully had disease enfeebled them.

The hospital at Hythe being filled with the sick, the barracks became a hospital, and as deaths ensued and thinned the wards, the men were continually removed, making a progress from barrack to hospital, and from hospital to the grave. The ward of the hospital in which I myself was, accommodated eleven men, and I saw, from my bed in the corner where I lay, this ward refilled ten times, the former patients being all carried out to the grave. I had been gradually removed as the men died, until I was driven up into a corner of the ward, where I lay, and had plenty of leisure to observe my comrades in misfortune, and witness their end. Some I beheld die quietly, and others were seized in various ways. Many got out of bed in a shivering delirium, and died upon the floor in the night-time.

Having been a shoemaker in the Rifles, I had saved during my service near two hundred pounds, which I had in the bank at Hythe at this time, so that I was enabled to procure extra wine and other nourishing things, and often gave my companions in misfortune a treat also; and this I think enabled my iron constitution to keep death so long at bay.

I saw one or two of my old Peninsula comrades, whom I had often seen fighting bravely in the field, die in this hospital in a miserable condition, their bodies being swollen up like barrels.

Everything was done for us that skill could devise, and nothing could exceed the kindness and attention of Dr Ridgeway towards us. Hot baths were brought into the hospital – and many a man died whilst in the bath.

I remember hearing, as I lay sick, that the firing over the graves of our comrades was dispensed with, the men died so fast; and when I got out, and went to the churchyard to look upon their graves I saw them lying in two lines there. As they in life had been enranked, so they lay also in similar order in death.

The medical men made every effort to trace the immediate cause of this mortality amongst us; and almost all the men were examined after death; but it was of no avail, as nothing could arrest the progress of the malady after it had reached a certain height. The doctor, I heard, generally attributed the deaths, in most cases, to enlargement of the spleen, as almost all were swollen and diseased in that part. I myself was dreadfully enlarged in the side, and for many years afterwards carried 'an extra paunch.'

As soon as the prospect began to brighten, and the men to recover a little, we managed to muster outside the hospital, some three hundred of us parading there morning and evening, for the benefit of fresh air; and medicine was served out to us as we stood enranked, the hospital orderlies passing along the files, and giving each man his dose from large jugs which they carried.

As we got better, an order arrived to furnish two companies of the second battalion and two companies of the third battalion, of Rifles, for Spain, as they were much wanted there. Accordingly an inspection took place, and two hundred men were picked out, all of whom were most anxious to go. I myself was rejected at that time as unfit, which I much regretted. However, on making application, after a few days I was accepted, principally on the recommendation of Lieutenant Cochrane, who much wished for me; and I, in consequence, once more started for foreign service.

From Hythe to Portsmouth, where we were to embark, was eight days' march; but the very first day found out some of the Walcheren lads. I myself was assisted that night to my billet, the ague having again seized me, and on the third day waggons were put in requisition to get us along the road. As we proceeded, some of those men who had relapsed died by the way, and were buried in different places we passed through. At Chichester, I recollect, a man was taken out of the waggon in which I myself lay, who had died beside me; and at that place he was buried.

At Portsmouth I remained one night, billeted with my fellow-travellers at the Dolphin. Here I was visited by an uncle who resided in the town; and who was much shocked at seeing me so much reduced, concluding it was impossible I could survive many days. Such was the sad state we were again reduced to. The next morning spring-waggons were procured for us, and we were sent back to Hilsea barracks for the benefit of medical advice; and I took a farewell of my uncle, expecting never to see him again. Such, however, was not to be the case, as out of the thirty-nine Riflemen who went into Hilsea hospital, I alone survived.

It may seem to my readers extraordinary that I should twice be the survivor of so many of my comrades. I can only, therefore, refer them to the medical men who attended us, if they yet live, Dr Ridgeway, of the Rifles, and Dr Fraser, who at that time was the surgeon at Hilsea.

I must not forget to mention an act of great kindness and humanity which was performed towards the soldiery whilst we lay sick at Hilsea hospital. Lady Grey, who, I believe, was the wife of the Commissioner of Portsmouth Dockyard at this time, was so much struck with the state of the sufferers, that she sent, one morning, two carts loaded with warm clothing for them; giving to each man, of whatsoever regiment, who had been at Walcheren, two pairs of flannel drawers and two flannel waistcoats. This circumstance was greatly appreciated by the men, and many, like myself, have never forgotten it.

After this, being the only Rifleman left at Hilsea, Lieutenant

Bardell made application to the general for leave for me to go into Dorsetshire to see my friends, which was granted; but the doctor shook his head, doubting I should ever be able to endure the journey. In about a week, however, I considered myself fit to undertake it; and, accordingly, a non-commissioned officer of one of the line regiments put me into a Salisbury coach. A lady and gentleman were my fellow passengers inside, and we started about four o'clock. They seemed not much to relish the look of a sick soldier in such close quarters; and, indeed, we had hardly cleared the town of Gosport before I gave them a dreadful fright. In short, I was attacked all at once with one of my periodical ague-fits, and shook to so desperate a degree that they were both horror-struck, and almost inclined to keep me company in my trembling. The lady thought that both herself and husband were lost, and would certainly catch the complaint; expressing herself as most unhappy in having begun her journey on that day. These fits generally lasted an hour and a quarter, and then came on a burning fever, during which I called for water at every place where the coach stopped. In fact, coachman, guard, and passengers, outside and in, by no means liked it, and expected every minute that I should die in the coach.

'Here's a nice go,' said the coachman, as he stopped at a place called Whitchurch, 'catch me ever taking up a sick soldier again if I can help it. This here poor devil's going to make a die of it in my coach.'

It seemed, indeed, as if I had personally offended the burly coachman, for he made an oration at every place he stopped at, and sent all the helpers and idlers to look at me, as I sat in his coach, till at last I was obliged to beg of him not to do so.

I had two attacks of this sort during the night, and was so bad that I myself thought with the coachman that I should never get out of the vehicle alive. Never, I should think, had passengers so unpleasant a journey as the lady and gentleman I travelled with.

At length, early in the morning, the coach stopped at a village one mile from my father's residence, which was on the estate of the present Marquis of Anglesey.* I had left my father's cottage quite a boy, and although I knew the landlord of the little inn where the coach stopped, and several other persons I saw there, none recognised me; so I made myself known as well as I could, for I was terribly exhausted, and the landlord immediately got four men to carry me home.

My father was much moved at beholding me return in so miserable a plight, as were also my stepmother and my brother. I remained with them eight months, six of which I lay in a hopeless state in bed, certificates being sent every month to Hythe stating my inability to move; and during which time Captain Hart sent four letters to the commanding officer, desiring I might be drafted out, if possible, to Spain, as, being a handicraft, I was much wanted there.

The medical men round the neighbourhood hearing of my state, many of them came to see me, in order to observe the nature of a complaint that had proved so fatal to our soldiers.

At the end of the eighth month (being once more somewhat recovered, and able to crawl about, with the aid of a stick, a few yards from our cottage door), as my stepmother had once or twice expressed herself burthened by this long illness, I resolved to attempt to return to my regiment. I was therefore transported in a cart to the King's Arms Inn, at Dorchester, my body being swollen up hard as a barrel, and my limbs covered with ulcers. Here the surgeons of the 9th and 11th Dragoons made an examination of me, and ordered me into Dorchester hospital, where I remained seven weeks; and here my case completely puzzled the faculty.

At length Dr Burroughs, on making his rounds, caught sight of me as I sat on my bed, dressed in my green uniform.

'Hallo! Rifleman,' he said, 'how came you here?'

Being told, he looked very sharply at me, and seemed to consider.

'Walcheren,' he inquired, 'eh?'

* This was the first Marquess, the hero of Waterloo. He did not die until 1854.

'Yes, sir,' I said, 'and it has not done with me yet.'

'Strip, my man,' he said, 'and lie on your back. What have you done for him?' he asked sharply of the doctor.

The doctor told him.

'Then try with him mercury, sir,' he said, 'both *externally* and *internally*.'

After saying which, in a rapid manner, he turned as quickly, and proceeded on his rounds amongst the rest of the patients.

I was now salivated most desperately, after which I got a little better, and resolved, at all hazards, to try and rejoin my regiment, for I was utterly tired of the hospital life I had altogether so long led. 'For Heaven's sake,' I said, 'let me go and die with my own regiment!'

With some little difficulty I got leave to go, and once again started, at my own expense, for Hythe, in Kent, by the coach. Before doing so, however, to my surprise, the medical man who had attended me under my father's roof, brought me in his bill, which was a pretty good one, amounting to sixty pounds! I thought this was pretty well for a poor soldier to be charged. Having still, however, enough left of my savings, I paid it; but I kept the bill, and afterwards showed it to Dr Scott of the Rifles, who remarked – 'It could not have been higher, Harris, if you had been a man possessing a thousand a year.'

When I made my appearance in the barrack-square at Hythe, I was like one risen from the dead; for I had been so long missing from amongst the few I knew there, that I was almost forgotten. A hardy Scot, named M'Pherson, was one of the first who recognised me.

'Eh, my certie,' he said, 'here's Harris come back. Why, I thought, man, ye was gane amangst the lave o' them, but the deil will na kill ye, I think!'

The day after my arrival I was once more in hospital, and here I remained under Dr Scott for twenty-eight weeks. Such was the Walcheren fever, and to this day I sometimes feel the remains of it in damp weather. From Hythe I was sent, amongst some other invalids, to Chelsea. Sixty of us marched together on this occasion. Many had lost their limbs, which, from wounds as well as disease, had been amputated; and altogether we did not make a very formidable appearance, being frequently obliged to be halted in the road to repair our strength, when the whole turn-out would be seen sitting or sprawling at full length by the wayside.

This march took us ten days to accomplish, and when we halted at Pimlico, we were pretty well done up. We were billeted in the different public-houses in Chelsea. With others, I lodged at the Three Crowns, close beside the Bun House.

I remember we paraded in the Five Fields, then an open space, but now covered with elegant mansions, and become a part of London. Three thousand invalids mustered here every morning – a motley group, presenting a true picture of the toils of war. There were the lame, the halt, and the blind, the sick, and the sorry, all in a lump. With those who had lost their limbs, there was not much trouble, as they became pensioners; but others were, some of them, closely examined from day to day as to their eligibility for service. Amongst others I was examined by Dr Lephan.

'What age are you, Rifleman?' he said.

'Thirty-two, sir,' I replied.

'What trade have you been of?' he inquired.

'A shoemaker,' I replied.

'Where have you been?' he said.

'In Denmark, Spain, Portugal, and Walcheren,' I said, 'in which latter place I met the worst enemy of all.'

'Never mind that,' he said, 'you'll do yet; and we will send you to a Veteran Battalion.'

Accordingly I was appointed to the 8th Veteran Battalion, with others, and sent to Fort Cumberland. Here I joined Captain Creswell's company – an officer who had lost one eye whilst in the 36th regiment in Spain.

I was again the only green-jacket of the lot, and the officers assembled round me during the first muster, and asked me numerous questions about my service amongst the Rifles, for we had a great reputation in the army at this time. Major Caldwell commanded the battalion; he had been in the 5th, and received a grievous wound in the head. He was a kind and soldier-like man, but if you put him out of temper you would soon find out that he felt his wound. Captain Picard was there too, and Captain Flaherty, and Lieutenant Moorhead; all of them were more or less shattered, whilst their men, although most of them were young, were very good specimens of war's stern service. One, perhaps, had a tale to tell of Salamanca, where he lost an eye, another spoke of the breach at Badajoz, where he got six balls at once in his body. Many paraded with sticks in their hands, and altogether it was something of a different sort of force to the active chaps I had been in the habit of serving amongst. In fact, I much regretted my green jacket, and grieved at being obliged to part with it for the red coat of the Veterans.

I remained in the Veterans only four months, as, at the expiration of that time, Napoleon was sent to Elba. We were then marched to Chelsea to be disbanded, where we met thousands of soldiers lining the streets, and lounging about before the different public-houses, with every description of wound and casualty incident to modern warfare. There hobbled the maimed light-infantry man, the heavy dragoon, the hussar, the artillery-man, the fusileer, and specimens from every regiment in the service. The Irishman, shouting and brandishing his crutch; the English soldier, reeling with drink; and the Scot, with grave and melancholy visage, sitting on the steps of the public-house amongst the crowd, listening to the skirl of his comrades' pipes, and thinking of the blue hills of his native land. Such were Chelsea and Pimlico in 1814.

In about a week's time I was discharged, and received a pension of sixpence per day; and, for the first time since I had been a shepherd lad on Blandford Downs, I saw myself in plain clothes, and with liberty to go and come where I liked. Before, however, my pension became due, I was again called upon to attend, together with others, in consequence of the escape of Bonaparte from Elba; but I was then in so miserable a plight with the remains of the fever and ague, which still attacked me every other day, that I did not answer the call, whereby I lost my pension. And here I may perhaps as well mention a slight anecdote of the Great Duke.

The Duke, I was told, observed in Spain that several men who had come out from England after Walcheren were unable to keep up on the march, and afterwards completely failed. He inquired the reason of this, and was told they were men who had been on the Walcheren expedition.

'Then never,' said the Duke, 'let another man be sent here who has been at Walcheren.'

At Fort Cumberland I remember another curious circumstance, which may, perhaps, in these times, be thought worthy of narration.

Many of the French prisoners had volunteered into the English service, and were formed into four companies, called the Independent Companies. These men were smart-looking fellows, and wore a green uniform, something like the Rifles. Whilst I was with the Veterans, one of these men deserted and was retaken at Portsmouth, and tried by court-martial at Fort Cumberland. Besides his crime of desertion he had aggravated it by gross insubordination, and he was accordingly sentenced to be flogged. We all, French and English, paraded to see the sentence carried into effect, and, in case of anything happening, and our opposite neighbours, the green-jackets, showing fight, the Veterans were all ordered to load with ball.

When the culprit heard the sentence read out to him he was a good deal annoyed, and begged that he might be shot as would have happened to him in his own country. Such, however, it was explained to him, could not be allowed, and he was accordingly punished. The Duke of York, who was then Commander-in-Chief, had thought it necessary to make this example, although all of us would have been glad to see him forgiven.*

Shortly after this, on Napoleon's being sent to Elba, these men were all liberated and sent home to their own country,

* Frederick Augustus, Duke of York (1763–1827). The second son of George III, he was appointed Commander-in-Chief in 1798.

with four pounds given to each man; and gloriously drunk they all were at Portsmouth the night they embarked.

The Veterans were very intimate and friendly with these Frenchmen as they were quartered together; and we were all sorry to hear (whether true or false I cannot say) that on their return, their uniforms betraying their having served us, they were grossly maltreated by their fellow countrymen.

Index

MILITARY HISTORY BOOKS

THE LETTERS OF PRIVATE WHEELER 1809–1828

An eyewitness account of the Battle of Waterloo
Edited and with a foreword by B. H. Liddell Hart
*'Vivid images – of people, landscape, events – flow from his
pen . . . one of military history's great originals'*
John Keegan
Paperback £9.99

THE DIARY OF A NAPOLEONIC FOOTSOLDIER
Jakob Walter

A conscript in the *Grande Armée's* account of the long march
home on the retreat from Moscow
Hardback £11.99 Illustrated

A SOLDIER OF THE SEVENTY-FIRST

The Journal of a Soldier in the Peninsular War
Edited and Introduced by Christopher Hibbert
*'His elegant style and his descriptive power take us
with him at every step.'*
The Sunday Telegraph
Paperback £9.99

GREAT BATTLES SERIES

AGINCOURT

Christopher Hibbert
Paperback £9.99 Illustrated

EDGEHILL

Peter Young
Paperback £15.99 Illustrated

CORUNNA

Christopher Hibbert
Paperback £14.99 Illustrated

HASTINGS

Peter Poyntz Wright
Paperback £10.99 Illustrated

WELLINGTON'S PENINSULAR VICTORIES

Michael Glover
Paperback £12.99 Illustrated

Order from THE WINDRUSH PRESS, LITTLE WINDOW, HIGH
STREET, MORETON-IN-MARSH, GLOS. GL56 0LL
MAJOR CREDIT CARDS ACCEPTED
TEL: 01608 652012 FAX: 01608 652125
£1 p&p within the UK